A

FEAR NOT!

Degree
is better than

A

Ph.D.

By
AIM OG

A TruBooks Publishing Book

Library of Congress Control Number: 2006901324

ISBN 0-9760009-6-2

Printed in the United States of America.
Distributed by Lightning Source Inc.

Acknowledgements

I wish to sincerely thank the Holy Spirit for inspiring me and guiding my heart and pen from the beginning to the final touches of this book. You are truly my best Friend: My God within.

I truly thank you

Dedicated

To God's People!

Contents

Introduction

Dear Reader:

I salute you! For you have made one of the greatest decisions of your life—**you purchased this book!** Now prepare yourself to defeat the greatest enemy ever known to man—this evil enemy the world refers to as Fear.

Historically, Fear has destroyed great people, great nations, and great civilizations. Fear is the same demon today as it was in our ancient yesterdays. And the interesting thing is—it has not lost any of its momentum! If anything, Fear seems to have gotten bolder, stronger, and incredibly is moving around a lot faster!

Moreover, all of this makes it of critical importance that one identify and eventually crucify this evil demon called fear.

Today, if a person is ill-equipped to control this brutal BEAST called Fear—he or she will simply be torn asunder. Fear is the most vicious beast on this planet! Fear kills men, women and children regardless of sex, age, race, color, class or creed.

Thus, you are very fortunate to have purchased this book because with it you will have the indispensable keys to completely destroy this evil power called *Fear!*

The inspiration for this book was to help all humankind yet it is mainly meant for our youth! For I pity the child who doesn't learn the essential principles of Fear early in his or her life. One chapter in this book is entitled, *"Fear: The Thing That Turned A Child Into A Champ!"* In it, I discuss my personal experience with Fear and how it haunted me for years until I was forced to confront it, combat it and eventually was able to defeat it! As I look back at those phobic periods of my childhood, I wish that there had existed a book like the one you currently have in your hands.

Well, Now There Is! This book was especially written and the vocabulary was carefully toned down so that even a child with very basic reading skills will be able to easily understand it! However, don't be fooled by the simplicity of its delivery. Although this book is simple enough for a child—it is truly deep enough for the most intelligent parent!

In this book, *A Fear Not Degree Is Better Than a Ph.D.*, the reader will learn that fear is not a word but an acronym! This fundamental principle is not being taught in our current education systems i.e., elementary, high schools, and universities throughout the world. And it was this apparent gap in their curriculums that provided the motivation for this book.

Fear is not being taught—schools are only teaching how to spell it! However, Fear will put an *evil spell* on you, and you won't be able to dispel it!

Therefore, I made a conscious decision to tailor this very complex subject matter to make it easily understandable to teenagers. Fear loves it that the education systems, the intelligentsia, the leaders, and parents neglect to teach the younger generation about the dangerous effects, powers, and influences of Fear. And I hope that after reading this book, you will conclude that the author has done a fantastic job where our school systems and leaders have failed to begin!

So, with no further delays, let's bite right into the meat of this book as we begin with chapter one *"Fear: A Public Announcement!"* I hope you enjoy and learn much at the same time. So, buckle up because you're in for an intellectual ride of your life!

-AIM OG-
Your *Fear Not!* Coach.

Chapter One

FEAR: A Public Announcement!

There are four types of men: First is the man, who has conquered all his fears. This is categorized as being free.

Second is the man, who is being paralyzed by fear yet knows not. This is categorized as slow death.

Third is the man, who is being paralyzed by fear and knows it! This is categorized as new life.

Fourth is the man, who is being paralyzed by fear but doesn't know that he doesn't know that he's being paralyzed—nor does he even care. This is categorized as pure death!

So, what category of a man or woman are you? **This Is A Public Announcement!**

Fear is a universal dilemma. It affects every human being on this planet! There is not one single person in this world who is exempt from Fear. No matter your age, whether young, middle-aged, or old—this will not *under* qualify you nor will it *over* qualify you from feeling the effects of Fear.

There is no specific age that will spare you from the effects of Fear. Moreover, there is no amount of education, or any type of political power, which will spare you from Fear. And it doesn't matter how rich you are—you don't have enough money to buy your way out of Fear.

Fear is indiscriminate! Fear has no biases or prejudices. It's not racist or sexist.

Although, man has made great strides in recent years in the fields of science and technology, he has yet to make any significant progress in defeating *Human Fear*. Yes, man's most advanced technology has sent him as far as the moon yet human fear has not budged two tenths of an inch here on earth! This same technology can send a message from the U.S. to Japan in seconds, yet Fear has been rapidly sending evil messages for 6,000 years and we've been emotionally shell-shocked ever since.

So, where is all this advanced, technological progress in the area of human Fear? Unfortunately, there is none! This is because, while we are so preoccupied with our outer space endeavors—Fear is busy paralyzing our planet to such an extent that people are fearful to move! Yes, we're so busy worrying about sending rockets, aircrafts, and instant messages while fear is *instantly* sending vast numbers of our people to their early graves.

Fear is a dilemma! Fear is universal! It is in your home, your marriage, your children. You can find it in your business, work or school. Fear is in you! It is a universal dilemma that somehow has made a very conscious and deliberate decision not to leave our planet. This means that Fear is a big problem and will always remain one!

Fear is an especially sizeable problem if you don't *think* it's a problem. It becomes worse when you have not *accepted it* as a problem. Yet it becomes even worse than that, when you have *rejected it* as a problem.

Contrary to popular belief, Fear is at the core of every problem within the human experience. Fear was at the core of every problem you have ever had. Fear is the core of the problem you are currently having, and it will continue to be for every problem you will have in the future.

Fear is a problem! The only real problems that humans are having are the ones that they constantly have with Fear.

The human mind is a brilliant, mathematical machine and is naturally designed to solve and resolve problems. Fear is mankind's greatest problem yet the human mind has yet to solve it!

Terror Therapy

We live in a world that chooses to give consenting adults baby-pacifiers called treatments in **therapeutic copism**. Personally, I have coined this term to mean a system of therapy, which advocates that we just learn how to cope with our fears but never to subdue them. Therapeutic copism advocates that *fear stays around or that you welcome fear into your home and treat it as permanent company; tell it to have a seat; offer it some coffee or something to drink and if fear doesn't have any place to stay, then there is an extra bed upstairs (in your mind)— therefore it can stay with you!* Well this kind of treatment is a serious problem and is theoretically, scientifically, and philosophically incorrect! The book you are reading, "*A Fear Not Degree Is Better Than A Ph.D.*", absolutely rejects this kind of treatment.

Fear is not company—on the contrary, it's an uninvited and unrelenting intruder. **Fear is an uncouth killer!** And you don't invite killers to come into your home to meet the wife and kids or the husband and kids. No, Fear is a merciless killer which should never be invited into one's home (mind).

However, if this intruder called Fear has already broken into your home (mind) and is holding you as hostage (prisoner) then you have to employ different approaches, clever techniques or combinations of them in order to have him violently removed! However, treatments in therapeutic copism do not come close to getting a person to comprehend Fear in this way. Therefore, the person remains a hostage in this prison system called Fear.

The main problem I have with therapeutic copism is that it expertly specializes in only treating the symptoms! We as a people have a terrible habit of applying treatment to symptoms. We are very quick to apply soaps and creams to acne problems as opposed to treating its source—the system within!

Therapeutic copism approaches the dilemma of Fear in very much the same way. Anxiety-doctors called psychologists, clinicians and/or therapists are obsessed with treating symptoms. They particularly like to use and/or advocate antidepressant medications. These are very popular and widely recommended medications intended to treat various levels of Fear, i.e., anxiety disorders, social phobic disorders, panic disorders, emotional depressions, and emotional stress disorders, etc.

For example, a person who has frequent panic attacks, the drug **paroxeine** is given to treat that problem. For a person who has a severe social phobia, the drug **benzodiazepines** is prescribed to treat that problem. For a person who has a generalized anxiety disorder (GAD), the drug **venlafaxine** is given to treat that problem. And if a person fears giving oral presentations, class speeches, business lectures, etc., the doctor may prescribe **a beta-blocker.** This is another drug given to keep a person's heart from pounding, hands from shaking, and other physical symptoms from developing.

Now, correct me if I'm wrong, but isn't this the way drug users' cope with their problems? The under-the-counter **illegal** drug user takes drugs to escape his or her realities of life. Yet the FDA federally-approved, over-the-counter **legal** drug user take drugs to escape his or her realities too.

Here's what the two people both have in common: First, they are both *drug users!* Second, they both use drugs to help them cope and *escape* their existing realities. Yet one can go to **jail** and the other can go **home!** Third, after these drugs wear off, their situations and realities, in both cases, will still be *unchanged*. And the fourth and most compelling reality, in both of these cases, is *the drug dealers* (suppliers) have become incredibly rich! Yet these innocent clients fall prey and remain both physically and mentally victimized. And the overall conclusion is that they both have been greatly taken advantage of and **Medication Was Clearly Not The Answer!**

Medication is nothing but an aspirin—it's a temporary relief. Again, once your medication wears off, your problem is still the same. A panic attack victim needs a resolution not a temporary solution. Medications only treat symptoms! Agoraphobia is a symptom; hypochondria is a symptom; paranoid schizophrenia is a symptom; a panic attack is a symptom. But what's the problem? What's the root of the problem? After all the medications and after all the treatments, the ultimate factor remains: *You Are Still Paralyzed By Your Own Personal Fears.* And in order for you to ever stand a chance of getting a true answer to your problem—you will need to go to its source and not to its symptom. In this case, the source lies in the mental department, which is none other than the human mind.

So, what is the mind? The mind is the seat of consciousness where your thoughts, intellect, feeling of emotions and perceptions all take place.

Fear is a mind science and a mind manipulation going on all at the same time. Our greatest problem with fear is that 99.9% of the people do not know how to define it.

Moreover, the thing that every man and woman must know is that the mind is a master problem-solver. However, if you cannot properly define the problem—your mind cannot possibly develop a solution. Just as a calculator cannot guesstimate what problem you want it to solve—you must input the right equation in order for you to get the right result. The mind works the exact same way, in that, if you give it the proper diagnosis—you will reap the correct prognosis. Yet if you give it the wrong diagnosis—you will reap the wrong prognosis. **Wrong diagnosis, wrong prognosis!** It is just as simple as that.

Treatment in therapeutic copism is the **wrong diagnosis**. And using medication as a remedy will provide the **wrong prognosis**. So, it is indeed vital that we correctly define Fear. However, you cannot have just any definition; you must have the correct one. Our biggest and greatest problem has been in the definition department. We have never correctly defined Fear. The car (which is the definition of fear) has not even been started. The key (the true answer to fear) has never been inserted into the ignition (the solution area). This is partly why we have not made any inroads in combating this beast called FEAR—because we have never gotten on the road!

Fear Is Big Business

It's no secret that investing in the business of building prison systems does have huge incentives. But to invest in building prison systems within the human mind has a far greater and even more profitable incentive.

Who has the most to gain from building these prison systems *within?* There are a lot of thoughts, programs, strategies, and governmental institutions specifically designed to put you in this human cage called Fear. And there are very calculative and manipulative reasons behind why these key players in government are obsessed with putting their people in the terror dome called Fear. You may ask why? It is because Fear breeds an extraordinary amount of profits! Fear is big money! **Fear Pays Big Time!** There are a lot of great benefits behind putting you in this institutional program called Fear.

Mentally, Fear starts off as software (a thought) then it converts into hardware (on your soul), and this is what makes it very difficult to drive away.

In our next chapter, you will see why world leaders are so obsessed with instilling this evil program within the inner systems of their own people. These world leaders have a set of rules and guidelines, which serve as their own and personal version of the Bible and it's entitled . . .

Chapter Two

FEAR:
The World's Ten Commandments!

1. *Thou shall Fear.*

2. *Thou shall fear even more.*

3. *Thou shall fear even more than that!*

4. *Thou shall fear all the time.*

5. *Thou shall fear forever.*

6. *Thou shall never get tired of fearing.*

7. *Thou shall fear every time thou get a chance!*

8. *Thou shall never <u>learneth</u> about Fear–for this will be a sin.*

9. *Fear is Lord.*

10. *Fear is your God.*

We live in a world of absolute Fear. Fear is King! Fear is Lord! And for too many people, Fear is their God! Fear is a controlling and very powerful factor in our world. Everything in our world promotes and is filled with Fear.

Fear, Fear, Fear is the order of the day! This is exactly how world leaders stay in power. The world powers have a **"Population Fear Control 12-Step Policy."** It must be enforced to the fullest extent, in order to rule you and everybody else in the world completely. These rules are as follow:

<u>Rule #1</u>: Establish Fear in the hearts of every man, woman, and child on this planet at all cost!

<u>Rule #2</u>: **The Same As Rule Number One!** And that is the same answer for **Rules 3 to 12.**

To instill Fear in the hearts of every man, woman, and child is the ONE and ONLY goal!

IN ORDER TO RULE YOU, the world leaders have to **first** put you into captivity or bondage. Fear is this bondage! There is absolutely no easier way to rule six billion people and to keep them all in total submission than by putting them in this bondage called Fear.

The world wants you to Fear anything and everything, i.e., fear life, death, democrats, republicans, communists, socialists, the judicial system, prison systems, taxes, bill collectors, the passing of a new law, I.R.S., judges, prosecutors, police, murderers, rapists, serial killers, cancers, tumors and A.I.D.S. Fear losing your job, fear being interviewed for a job, and become more fearful when you finally get the job. Fear success, fear failure, fear driving in cars, fear flying in planes.

We are programmed to fear, fear, fear! Can we ever get enough of Fear? Well, that is the overall plan of the **World Powers.** It is to never allow the people to get enough of the terror of Fear—I MEAN NEVER!!! You will never get anywhere in Fear! Fear shuts down and paralyzes all of your movements, i.e., your physical, mental and spiritual movements! But where does Fear come from? Well, our next chapter will attempt to shed some light on this question and it's entitled...

Chapter Three

FEAR Starts From The Cradle!

The first form of **Fear** children experience is the first time their parents leave them alone. A child will go into absolute convulsions, as he or she begins to scream out violently. Here is what a parent experiences when leaving a child all alone in a room:

"Immediately, the child will begin to scream hysterically, the little heart will begin to beat very rapidly, blood pressure will skyrocket abnormally, hands will become clammy and sticky, eyes will become blood-shot, and the little mouth will start shivering uncontrollably. And yet all of this wild, out-of-control and neurotic activity will come to a SCREECHING HALT once a parent reenters the room! You would have thought this child had just lost its damn mind!"

Well, the point is not that the child has lost his or her mind. This was just the child's first experience and rude introduction to the very merciless demon called **Fear.**

What happened here was that, in the child's mind, it appeared that the only sense of protection was lost when mom or dad stepped out the room. The perception of lack of protection was the basis of this **Fear!** The parents were this child's only umbrella of protection—so when the umbrella moved (walked) away, the ultra-violet rays of **Fear** began to radiate on this child at such a neurotic rate that it caused the child to undergo a tremendous state of shock, commonly referred to as **Fear**. Thus, separation from parents or other persons whom the child is close to is a child's first lesson on the effects of **Fear**.

This experience with **Fear** has taught the child another "F-word" called *Fortitude*. Fortitude came as a result of Fear as the child was seriously threatened by the perception of not having it. Consequently, this completes this child's identification of the early stages of the five F's in life, which are as follows:

(1) **Family:** A child recognizes parents or care takers.
(2) **Food:** A child recognizes what satisfies hunger.
(3) **Fluids:** A child recognizes what satisfies thirst.
(4) **Fear:** A child recognizes emotional endangerment.

(5) **Fortitude:** A child recognizes security from emotional endangerment.

Chapter Four

The "*Let'em Scream*" Technique

This indoctrination was never a part of formal education—parents somehow just naturally picked this up out of pure frustration! *The let'em scream* technique is a very popular parental technique that is applied all over the world. It is an attempt to wear the child down until the child gets so tired of screaming that he or she eventually just falls asleep.

The only problem I have with *The let'em scream* technique is that 99.9% of all parents are not applying this technique effectively. Parents are most concerned with putting a swift end to their child's constant yelling and screaming by any means necessary.

However, *The let'em scream* method, when done properly, will teach the child an invaluable lesson on overcoming **Fear.** *The let'em scream* method should simply say:

"*My child, I love you, but you're going to have to understand that mommy has a lot of other things that she has to do around the house for your benefit, and I* can't take you everywhere I go. So, there is no need to Fear. For you are protected even when you cannot see me—trust me. As you are the most precious person in my life and nothing—I mean nothing—comes before you."

When a child becomes accustomed to mommy or daddy leaving them alone (in a room)—this means that the child has intelligently understood every nonverbal word that its mother or father has said to them through The "let 'em scream" method of communication.

The let 'em scream method is not about trying to wear a child down emotionally—but on the contrary, it's about very intelligently beginning and building a bonding relationship. This very delicate relationship, if nurtured properly, will solidify a strong connection.

The let 'em scream method of communication should affirm and reaffirm the love, trust, protection, and unbreakable bond between parent and child. And parents must apply this method solely for this outcome. In fact, if this is NOT the intended purpose, any other purpose is vitally insignificant!

The *scream* itself is the child's best form of communication. Every scream from an infant or child is a message, which must be understood. As a parent, you must learn how to receive and respond appropriately. No communication should be neglected especially that of an infant or child.

Therefore, when a child uncontrollably screams out every time mommy or daddy leaves the room, then this child is having a fear of abandonment-problem. This is true for every child during this period of development.

At this stage, all children have **fear of abandonment-problems,** which can be identified as a child's first form of fear. It begins in the cradle where a child experiences his or her first introduction to this evil demon called Fear. Also, yet very unfortunately, this will be the last time that an attempt will be made to teach this child the reasons why he or she should not *fear* this ugly demon called Fear.

Henceforth, the child will enter into a world where he or she will learn *copism* methods on how to deal with this demon, which will be discussed, in later chapters.

For the most part, this will not be this child's last time putting up a scream in the fear of abandonment-department. Meaning what? Meaning, as a child gets older, he or she will encounter other moments in life when fear of abandonment will be an issue. Yet this time it will have nothing to do with: *Where are my parents?* But it will have everything to do with: *Where is my Higher Power?*

So, trust that there will be another SCREAM of a different kind but the VICTIMIZER will be the same! Therefore, it behooves you to not be indifferent about your child's screams because there will be times when you, too, will desperately call out to your Higher Power and you would not want this Higher Power to be indifferent to your outcry (if you haven't had this outcry already!).

Thus, the purpose of this chapter is to explain the fear-dynamics behind the infamous *"let 'em scream"* phenomenon. Also, to point out that children are not screaming their lungs out just because they don't want you to leave; they are undergoing the greatest fear they have ever experienced in their lives: **Fear of Abandonment.** So Please Take These Screams Seriously.

Remember, it is in the cradle that a child experiences one of the greatest levels of fear. But who and what will prepare this child for one of the greatest levels of fear in his or her **Adult Life?** This leads us to our next chapter entitled...

Chapter Five

FEAR:
The World's Greatest Serial Killer!

There is no one who has killed more people on this planet than the killer commonly known as *Fear*. Fear has killed many great nations, great civilizations, and a whole lot of great people.

Fear doesn't seem to be losing any of its momentum even to this very day. If anything, Fear seems to have picked up its pace! Fear is a constant killer. According to the American Institute of Stress, it is reported that all leading causes of death, including heart diseases, cancers, accidents, and suicides are related to emotional stress, which in effect is nothing but Fear.

Fear is the world's greatest serial KILLER and it is on a terrifying and vicious rampage!

Fear is on a silent, genocidal tour seeking and attacking anyone it can devour! Fear is on a mission. Fear and A.I.D.S are having a killing contest! But Fear is winning by an enormous landslide!

Fear is callous; it is ruthless. The world's most dangerous serial killers have killed due to certain inborn ethnic, racial, political, cultural, religious, prejudices and/or biases. Yet the serial killer commonly known as Fear has killed well over a billion more people without a strain of prejudice. Fear killed all these innocent people without a conscience. Fear is renowned for killing without a conscience because it uses your conscience instead!

Fear is this thing that kills you gradually. Fear kills you softly, but definitely—Fear will kill you *for surely!* Fear has killed many innocent people and still Fear has not been brought to justice! Fear must have its day in court—Universal Court!

Chapter Six

FEAR vs. The Education System!

The universal referee declares, *"And the winner by technical, critical, brutal, fatal, lethal, suicidal, homicidal, genocidal KNOCK OUT–and still the undisputed, undefeated champion of the world–your own personal **Fear!**"*

The education systems, both public and private, are the worst training facilities for the battle of personal fear on the face of this earth! It is disgusting, how even armed with a master's degree, you are no better prepared to deal with human fear than an eighth grade drop out! The person with the master's degree and the eighth grade drop out both have one thing in common: they are in the same class, sharing the same books, and doing the same homework assignments in the universal class of Fear.

I would be totally remiss if I didn't speak to our other fine group of intellectual elite–those who have Ph.D.'s. Sad to say, this esteemed group of intellectuals is no better prepared to deal with human fear than the rest of the world. The person with the Ph.D. has all this impressive education, many graduated with outstanding honors yet Fear still succeeds in crippling and negating this person, in spite of educational prestige. **Hmmm, some education you have!** Yeah, you have a Ph.D. but you're scared to death of a kindergarten word like Fear! You are like a brand new car, all ready to travel the world, but you do not have the key (to Fear) so you can't go anywhere because *you are too damn scared!*

Our school systems, even at the college levels, have truly failed us in the area of *defining, discerning and dealing* with this evil demon called Fear. How could you have graduated with a doctoral degree in anything and still not be mentally equipped to masterfully handle a word which you have been spelling and pronouncing since elementary school?

However, you are not to blame. I blame the educational system, which really did not prepare you to fight and defeat this powerful inner enemy. The terrible thing about it all is that this very same educational system is still not teaching our new students on how to effectively *define, identify, and nullify,* the power of Fear. Thus, we stand a chance of developing another crop of graduates with bachelor's, master's and Ph.D.'s who will still come up short in *defining, identifying, and nullifying* the power of Fear just like the graduating class that preceded them.

How is it possible that a person can go from K-12 and over four years of college with a bachelor's, master's or Ph.D. and still be unable to properly define human Fear? A master's degree or a Ph.D. is just too much time and money spent for one to be unable to define a simple word like Fear.

Moreover, if you were to ask one hundred master's and/or Ph.D. recipients to define fear—ninety nine percent of them would get it wrong! Fear cannot be summed up with the few lines dedicated to it in the dictionary. Fear deserves its very own *unabridged, personal dictionary!*

In our curriculum system, Fear needs to be as vitally important as the three R's, i.e., reading, "riting," and "rithemetic." Our educational system should mandate reading, "riting," "rithmetic" and *Fear!* Meaning, if you do not do well on your test scores in the area of Fear you will stay back or will not graduate to the next grade level. It's just as simple as that, because in the real world of life, you will stay back anyway! You will stay back in your mental, spiritual, personal, emotional, family-oriented, and business-oriented development.

Due to your lack of knowledge of Fear—you won't know how to deal with the intense level of anxiety that comes from terrible moments in your life, such as bankruptcy or losing your only job.

You will crack under this level of stress because you have never been taught how to properly manage human Fear under these circumstances. So, again, you will stay back and experience major setbacks anyway.

Therefore, it would be better if you had stayed back a grade-level with a chance to get it right the following year than stay back in the real world of life and not have the chance to get it right without having it cost you and your family a major mental breakdown due to the emotional pressures of Fear.

The reason why I addressed the issue about academic degrees earlier was not to bash or belittle them but only to show that you are not assured success even with an associate, bachelor's, master's or even a Ph.D. because Fear is a whole new other animal! There needs to be an independent four-year accredited college, exclusively educating people about the effects of Fear called *Fear University.*

Fear Universities should spread through out every city, state, country, and the world over. If and when you graduated from one of these universities—you would be fully and completely qualified for success and would have the ability to tackle any and every confrontation with Fear. Fear is the only obstacle of life that will stand in your way in an attempt to stop, maim and destroy you.

Fear is this bully, demon, and destroyer that the universities of the world didn't prepare you for. It is because they thought that Fear, whose REAL name is the devil, was just a religious thing! Yes, these professors have even convinced you that these inescapable demons on the road to success were only myths and just plain old spiritual doctrine! So you thought you were really prepared for a life that you knew nothing about while armed only with a few *dollars, a desire, and a degree.* You honestly thought that you were really prepared for the big, bad duke in the road—this demon, this devourer and destroyer called Fear, which every man, woman, and child must inescapably face.

Yeah, this bully is so terribly crude, evil, and relentless that he has even made many devout atheists convert and become believers of God or at least made them call out His Name! Yes, this *real* bully, properly known as Fear, is just that bad!

However, if you are an atheist and you're seeking counseling on Fear, commonly called depression or anxiety, then you are seeking a higher power. You are seeking, whether you know it not, for God. It's a fact, anytime you are searching for a power beyond the confines of the **self** then you are searching for God. You want to know God; you want to know about his powers and whether he can help YOU. And the All-Forgiving and Universal Answer is Yes! God can and will help you but you should never deny the existence of His powers in the name of atheism or any other **ism**.

This Higher Power is not in your local community or even in the offices of your best group of psychiatrists or stress management therapists. Oh no, for they have **Fear-problems** too! So, where do they go when they have to deal with their phobias? The undeniable answer is, "*they seek the power that is above and beyond the confines of the **self** and there is no other power in this entire universe that is able to do such but the power of God.*

Fear is your personal enemy and it is the greatest enemy you will ever face in your life! There is no such thing as several enemies or obstacles in life. There is only **one** enemy and **one** obstacle in life and religious people call it the devil. This very same devil goes by a whole lot of other clever names such as Fear, anxiety, worry, nervousness, stress, depression, doubt, apprehension, intimidation, panic-attacks, scariness, butterflies, lack of confidence, low self-esteem, liar, demon, devourer, destroyer, Satan, Lucifer, fake, phony, murderer, robber, stealer, cheater, and hundreds of other names.

This devil is the same enemy; he just takes on many different disguises under many different names! However, his nature has not changed at all! Fear is the enemy, the greatest enemy you will ever face in your entire life! Fear is nothing but the devil going by a different name. The devil is nothing but *lived* spelled backwards! As long as you are living in Fear—you are living backwards! Fear is the greatest and only enemy you will ever face in your life. I Stake My Life On It!!!

Please Don't Let The Many Names Fool You For The Enemy's Nature and Purpose Is Still The Same: **To Steal, Kill and Destroy You!** The Enemy

Wears Many Different Outfits (Names) But Trust Me—It Is The Same Spiritual Individual (Evil Force!).

Chapter Seven

FEAR: A Mind Science

In this chapter, we will be discussing the positive and negative aspects of Fear. However, let us start off by making it very clear that there is nothing positive about Fear (the devil) except the time when you finally defeat it! And what a glorious time that will be! Your victory over Fear is when all your fears are totally within your control. Absolute fear-control is within your reach, ability, and power but it all takes place in the mind!

The power of the mind is an amazingly awesome inner-power! It is only an extension of a much greater source of power called God power. The universe—an outlet of God's power and from where the mind draws its power—is an incredible and supremely superior powerhouse. It enlightens and produces electricity to service the entire electrical needs of planets, moons, stars and galaxies! There are a whole lot of components: electrons, neutrons, and protons that make up two superior powers called positivity and negativity.

The positive and negative forces of life are the only two powers in the universe! It is impossible for the universe to work without these two super powers. In fact, the universe would be out of business if only **one** of these powers were in operation. The point is . . . the universe needs them both to showcase its incredibly awesome beauty, power, and force. The universe is stunningly beautiful yet it would have not been able to "cosmically strut its stuff" if it were not for the positive and negative forces of life.

The universe, our true mother nature, figured out a way to use both positive and negative forces to *power* her brand new business of operating in the physical, mental, and spiritual realms of life! Everything in the universe depends on both of these forces of life.

The earth would not be able to spin as fast as it does were it not for the positive and negative forces.

The moon and stars would not be able to shine as the bright lamps in universal darkness were it not for positive and negative forces.

The sun, a gigantic ball of fire, serves as a radiator that is responsible for heating, giving life, providing vitamins, minerals, and other essential nutrients to our solar system.

Land, a fertilized soil, is made of positive and negative components that energize a seed so that it will be able to produce food for the sustenance of life.

A man's brain is his **land** and the mind of man is his **soil**. This mind (soil) has both positive and negative components (forces) that will energize (develop) his seed (thought) so that it will be able to produce food (an enriched state of mind). However, all of this would come to a halt if were not for the positive and negative forces of life.

Fear is this negative energy that you must use for your positive benefit! In its original state, negative power is raw and very naked in nature. Negative energy is nothing but a body of negative power that must be given a name! You just cannot allow a thing to go for thousands of years without giving it a name. This power has to be called something!

Everything in nature has a label or a name and if it doesn't have one—man will immediately give it one! The names of things in nature are meant for us to personally identify with them and/or to be able to describe them to others. **So, names or the custom of naming is a good natural**

practice for identification purposes! There are certain things in life that—although you cannot physically see them—you still must give them a name, so that you may be able to identify them!

This is true in the case of *negative energy*. You will never be able to physically see it so, you definitely need a word to be able to identify it. It is unfortunate that this type of power (negative power) has historically been given so many other names but the most popular is the religious term **devil**. There are other names just as popular, such as Satan, Lucifer, Serpent, and Demon. However, this very same negative energy disguises itself by many other clever names as anxiety, stress, worry, doubt and the ever-popular Fear. Fear is the widely used name to describe the very nature of this negative power. Yet all of these names are nothing but the many attributes of this same energy called negativity.

The Negativity of Fear

Negativity means **negative activity!** All of the names and attributes of this negative power produce negative activity. Fear brings about negative activity; anxiety brings about negative activity; stress brings about negative activity; worry brings about negative activity; doubt brings about negative activity, and all of these negative activities happen within the confines of an active mind.

Fear is your greatest negative force going up against your greater positive power: *the positive power within*. The devil is Fear and Fear is the devil. The devil is negative and negative is Fear.

The devil, properly known as negative power, electrically wars against God—properly known as positive power. These two great powers are universal opposites! Allow me to explain how these two dynamic forces work: God causes things to **live**; the devil causes things to **evil**. The word *live* must interchangeably reverse in order to distinguish one force of power from another. The negative current (fear) is only meant to start (motivate) your engine (purpose) and not meant to shut it off (paralyze it!).

Fear is this negative force that can be used for your positive benefit! Here is how it works: first, you have to be a person who has a firm resolution that *anything you can conceive–you can achieve!* Let's say you want to accomplish something BIG in life, which many would consider an insurmountable task. Yet you're convinced that it can be done and you are the one that can do it! However, for some strange reason, you cannot seem to get yourself motivated to do it. Then comes the devil (or negative force), which says to you: *"Hmmm, you will never–I mean NEVER be able to do it! First of all, you are a woman in a man's world. Secondly, you really don't come from the best family; your mother is a chronic alcoholic and your father is a loser and strung out on drugs. Plus, you're raising three kids on your own and you didn't even finish college. But more importantly YOU'RE FAT!"* Okay, now the motivation has just kicked into full gear–in other words IT'S ON!!! The once seemingly I-CAN'T-GET-MYSELF-MOTIVATED big task has now been turbocharged for pure action!

Although this big task was positive, productive, and something that you desperately wanted in life–you just couldn't seem to get inspired to work towards it. However, negative energy (the devil) did what by nature it was designed to do which was to discourage, and get you to blame yourself, blame others, make all types of excuses. Ultimately, its goal was to get you to project a negative outcome! Fortunately, you did not give in to the negative suggestions or power of Fear.

Here, you have used your negative force for your positive benefit! You have learned how to channel your negative energy as motivation for your positive good, which will then turn on your *light switch*, your *success switch*, your *prosperity switch* for a positive result! However, many of us do not know how to use our negative force as motivation to fuel our goals for our positive benefits. So, instead of using our negative forces to motivate, many of us instead allow them to totally hinder us!

It takes both the positive and the negative to make things work. You will never be able to turn on a light with just one electrical current. Man and woman need both the positive and negative forces of life to activate their pursuits and goals in life. Fear is a negative force and we must learn how to use this force and not be abused by it!

Jesus said, "*For, my strength is made perfect in weakness (2 Corinthians 12:9).*" Here, Jesus was saying that my POSITIVITY is made perfect in my NEGATIVITY. Your strength is your faith; your weakness is what you fear. Thus, use your FEAR to empower your FAITH.

Chapter Eight

FEAR and The Road To Riches!

The Body is the vehicle: Car.

Fear is the negative (-) bolt.

Faith is the positive (+) bolt.

The Soul is the battery.

Truth is the headlight.

The Mind is the steering wheel.

Holy Spirit is the motivation: Gas.

Desired Destination: God's Heaven!

Chapter Nine

FEAR Is Just Spiritual Electricity!

In this chapter, I will explain the three components of a natural power that assist in producing spiritual electricity as designed by the Creator. These three negative components are absolutely essential for human development.

These tri-part components of spiritual electricity are classified as the *meat*, the *fat* and the *bone*. The *meat*, the *fat* and the *bone* are electrical brain-forces that conduct all their business in the mind of man. Out of these three components, the part referred to as the meat is properly called FEAR and is by far the most deadliest!

Therefore, we must learn how to de-activate and de-emphasize the effects of Fear—by that I mean, we must learn how to convert Fear into just raw, naked electricity! How do you do that? This can be done by cutting away the *meat* and the *fat* and leaving nothing but the *raw bone*!

Negativity is the *raw bone*. **Fear** is the *meat* which coarsely wraps around it. The **fat** is *lies, anxiety, stress, nervousness, scariness, weariness and any* *other mess that ends with* <u>ness</u>! So, when you cut away the *meat and fat*—you will get ***raw electricity,*** which is all that is needed for spiritual electricity and the purpose of balancing one's righteousness!

The word *sin* means *Spirit In Negativity.* When the human soul is operating or living in **sin,** it is operating or living in **negative activity.** Yet all negative activity comes from the negative current, which is spiritual electricity that incubates human sins.

There are universal penalties you will receive when your spirit is operating in negative activity. However, these spiritual offenses are beneficial and remedial for your spiritual development. All humans need to be constantly reminded of the consequences for their sins and this is one of the main purposes of the negative current.

Furthermore, if you are unaware or oblivious to the consequences of sin, you will have no regard or respect for the order and law of universal righteousness. The law of consequences is the law commonly referred to as *the law of Karma.* It serves the purpose of allowing you to reap the benefits of what you sow. If you plant good seeds then you will reap good results, but if you plant bad seeds then beware of bad results.

The only thing we need from this negative current is the *raw electricity*, which it brings. This means we must discard the **meat** and the **fat,** (i.e., *fear, anxiety, stress, lies, etc.,*) and just go straight to the **naked bone!**

What does this mean? **The fatty meat** is the *fear, the deceptions, the illusions, the false evidence, the lies, etc.* When Fear attempts to scare you from pursuing a positive goal—this should only inspire you more! This type of thinking is called going straight to the **bone!**

The bone has juice soaked in it from the evil meat known as Fear. The juice (negative energy) is only meant to juice you up (motivate you!) You must reject **the fatty meat** (i.e. *the fears, the deceptions, the illusions, the false evidence, the lies, etc.*) and just extract the juice from **the bone** (or negative energy) and mix it with your positive energy in order to produce your positive result! Remember, a light bulb needs both positive and negative currents in order for it to work.

Are we not children of the light? Of course we are. Jesus said, "*Ye are the light of the world (Matthew 5:14).*" What kind of light do you know of that does not use a negative current? The answer to that question is simply—there isn't any!

Every light in our universe uses a negative power in cooperation with positive power in order to make it shine. So, every man and woman must follow this same law: using their negative power with their positive power in order to make themselves spiritually shine!

This is a universal law and as long as you are still a product of the universe then this same law applies to you, too! However, you must understand that just because we use negative power with positive power—it does not mean that we will get a negative result. This is the same as a lamp that uses both negative and positive power. We must learn how to use those things that are meant to destroy us and use them to help, build, develop and strengthen us. This is exactly what Jesus meant when he said to us: "*My strength is made perfect in my weakness.*" Jesus was clearly teaching that his strength (positive power) was made perfect by the temptation of the devil (his negative power). In this, Jesus is saying to us, we must learn how to use those things that are meant to destroy us like fear, anxiety, stress, weariness, emotional disorder, etc., and use them to help, build, develop and strengthen us.

The people who are experts at using negative energy to act, move, and respond for a positive good I call "*electri-tarians.*" You may ask, *what is an electri-tarian?* An *electri-tarian* is one who uses his negative power to blend perfectly with his positive power in order to brew a stew of success!

An *electri-tarian* is one who knows how to use, dissect and disorient Fear in order to get to the real purpose behind it, which is to strengthen one's character! *Vegetarians* do not eat **meat** but *electri-tarians* do not eat the **emotional-meat** called Fear.

An electri-tarians avoids the essential components of this negative power. This negative power is originally *spiritual* and is then transposed as *emotional* then is labeled and packaged and given the name *FEAR.*

An electri-tarian is one that uses negative energy for spiritual purposes only! An *electri-tarian* knows that once his inner lamp is turned on—he will then be able to spiritually see all the dark areas in his life that he could not see before—namely, all those little hiding places of fear and all its evil associates, i.e., anxiety, stress, worry, doubt, apprehension, etc. So, an *electri-tarian* doesn't care for the *meat or fat*. Moreover, an *electri-tarian* doesn't trim the *meat or fat* because that will mean that this person is coping with the *meat and fat*.

To cope means to compromise.

If you are compromising with the *meat* then this means you have tenderized this *meat,* making it fit to be eaten or consumed. So, don't listen to anyone who says to you, "*You need to cope with your fears!*" To cope is to compromise and to compromise is to tenderize. When you tenderize your meat—you are planning on compromising, settling, and accepting your meat (fear) as a delicacy: A FRIEND!

So, don't tenderize this meat called Fear. Instead, become an *electri-tarian,* so that you can finally start to brightly see the dark areas of your beautiful world: Life. Truly, you will never really start living until you have finally stop fearing. Fear can make your whole world appear dark but not to an *electri-tarian because*—He'll Use This Negative Energy To Light It Up!!!

Remember what Jesus said: *"Ye are the light of the world."* **So, go shine in it!**

Chapter Ten

The True Meaning of Fear

Question:

What is Fear?

Answer:

False

Evidence

About

Reality!

(Which Falsely Envisions Agonizing Results)

Chapter Eleven

The Explanation of F.E.A.R.

Fear is not a word; it's an acronym! Fear is simply *False Evidence About Reality!* There is nothing *real* about Fear, until the moment you think there is! Fear paints false images, false pictures, false projections of assumed realities. Fear is the master of assumption. Fear will make an *ass* out of *u* and *me* very constantly and consistently!

As Faith is the evidence of things not seen; Fear is false evidence of things not seen! Faith tells the truth, while Fear tells the lie. Faith is the good and truthful prophet that always projects the truth, while Fear is the evil false prophet that always projects the lie.

Faith is the positive; Fear is the negative. They both work together—although, they really don't like each other. However, they both manage to **work along** even though they really don't **get along**.

Faith is good and healthy nutrition while Fear is bad and worse than junk food. Faith can make you truly healthy, while Fear will make you terribly sick!

Fear is the master of deception—the world's greatest deceiver! Fear is the devil going by another name. Fear is evil—plus, it tells many lies. The greatest lie Fear ever told was that Faith was an absolute lie!

Fear is *False Evidence About Reality which Falsely Envisions Agonizing Results!* The primary order of business is for Fear to falsely envision agonizing results. There's no other way to intimidate, terrify or petrify you than to falsely project to you a painful and uncomfortable outcome. Certainly, if you have been convinced of an agonizing result it will create fear within you.

But where does Fear come from? It starts when you conclude that you are *incapable* of preventing a particular hurt, harm or agonizing result whether physically, mentally, spiritually and/or emotionally!

People do not fear anything that they know they can prevent from causing them harm! People only fear the things they *believe* they cannot prevent from harming them! Notice how the word *believe* has to come into play in order for fear to be effective!

Fear needs an accomplice to partner with this deception! Fear cannot be effective without *Mr. Believe's* participation! And your belief system has been carefully chosen to participate in this hateful self-crime!

Fear cannot be effective without working closely with the human belief system! Once a person *believes* that something has the ability to hurt them and that they cannot prevent such harm—the formula called Fear is instantly created.

In competitive sports, athletes fear the thought of losing because their *belief systems* are not convinced that they can prevent it. In business, a man or woman fears failure because their *belief systems* are not convinced that they can prevent it. In relationships, many men or women fear the thought of their loved ones cheating on them because they really cannot prevent it!

Any harm, hurt or pain that your *belief system* is not yet convinced that it can prevent—it will create or develop a fear for it.

If you look at the things you do not Fear—you will notice that you do not have a fear for those things only because your **natural survival and/or defense intuition** has already examined, estimated, and calculated how to prevent it!

For instance, if a four year old child were to say to you, "*I'm gonna beat you up!*" In this example, a man or woman's **natural survival and/or defense intuitive** program would not be intimidated by today's assignment—whatsoever! I mean, come on! Can you really go into a critically fearful state of shock due to a threat coming from a four-year-old child?

Hmmm, today's assignment doesn't stand a chance of stirring up your anxiety-juices nor does it pose a threat that your **natural survival and/or defense intuitive** program need be concerned with at all!

The human defense mechanism—known as one's **natural survival and/or defense intuitive** program—is a very complex process or "circumstance-calculator." I like the term *circumstance-calculator* because that is exactly what this program is! Meaning, it calculates circumstances to determine your abilities to escape harm. When the **natural survival and/or defense intuitive** program is unable to compute any means of escape—one will be neurotically welcomed to the world of Fear!

The fear-product is developed by what scientists call your nerves. The nervous system actually receives data from the bank of what you believe and it then creates a chemical potion based on this belief system. For the most part, if the nervous system decides your impending circumstance to be a joke or non-threatening in nature—it will produce a potion commonly referred to as laughter. You will begin to chuckle at this so-called imminent threat.

However, if your belief system didn't do a fine job of convincing your nerves that there was a prevention or an escape capability—then a very different brain-chemical will be created based on this shady and shaky belief system. And presto, the emotion called Fear is the end result!

The fundamental principle of Fear is this: "Where There Is No Prevention—There Will Be Apprehension."

So, if you cannot PREVENT it—you will INVENT it! Our next chapter will colorfully go into details and it is entitled...

Chapter Twelve

Fear is Self-Imprisonment!

Fear is a self-imprisonment: a personal bondage. When people fear they are voluntarily accusing, sentencing, and locking themselves up for a crime that they didn't commit (or perhaps did commit!). **In either case, it is self-incrimination!**

Many people play this stupid court game with themselves. Meaning, you have people who are so bold and cocky, that they will retract their own acknowledgment of having done something. Then they start convincing themselves that: *"Hey, maybe I didn't do it?"* As if the **self** doesn't know anything about what just happened! This is first degree INSANITY! In case you have missed the news bulletin (originally carved out 5,026 years ago on a rock)—IT READ: **You Cannot Fool Yourself!** But the weird thing is that there are so many people who are not quite convinced that this is true. These same people are still waiting for some scientific study to corroborate their theories.

Fear is personal entrapment. You can become so psychologically trapped in the web of your own personal fears that it will render you helplessly captive in the prison system of your mind. Consequently, this is the basic foundation of one's enrollment in the prison system called Fear.

Fear is the warden that runs this entire operation! Your **brain** is the institution; your **mind** is the cell that stores all the institutional rules of this prison system and **YOU** are the prisoner!

As the warden of this institution, Fear is responsible for imprisoning every soul on the face of this earth and anxiety, worry, doubt, afraid, scared, nervous, etc., are its prison guards.

However, there is a very strange thing about this type of prison system that is mind-boggling. Meaning, it populates itself! People actually raise their hands and volunteer to come to this type of prison. This is the only prison system where the prisoners (people) **prosecute, convict,** and then **sentence** themselves to lifetime sentences with NO PAROLE!

The institution of Fear is not a correctional facility but rather an *"incorrectional"* facility. Fear never intends for you to correct yourself in its facilities. Oh no, this is not the type of operation that Fear is running.

Fear is hell-bent on making you as incorrect with yourself as humanly possible. It is your sole responsibility to try to correct yourself in this evil institutional world—now, properly referred to as your MIND.

Fear is not trying to make you a law-abiding and fearless citizen—no, that would mean that you had been rehabilitated! Fear's purpose is to do the exact opposite. Fear wants to make you very scared and an extremely fearful citizen whether you are law-abiding or not.

A very interesting paradox is that Fear is not concerned with you being law-abiding as it is with you being **fearful** in the process! Fear's infamous motto is:

"Be whatever you want to be,

but just be fearful in the process!

Do whatever you want to do,

but just honor my name."

You can be a doctor just *fear acts of malpractice;*

You can be a lawyer just *fear being sued;*

You can be a high school teacher just *fear being shot!*

"*Be whatever you want to be,*
but just be fearful in the process!
You can do whatever you want to do,
but just honor my name. "

The moment Fear enters your mind it changes your mental and physiological system. Whatever you were trying to do has been overridden by this new program. Wherever you were planning to travel has just been replaced by this New Order.

Fear is a prison system on wheels! Your legs are its wheels. Therefore, Fear will go *wherever* you go, *whenever* you go and *however* you go. Yet its intentions are not to compliment your goals or plans—Fear's intentions are to disturb them!

Your own personal fears make you an inmate within the prison system that you unknowingly built for yourself. And the new chief-in-charge (thanks to you)—is Fear.

Fear, who is officially and properly referred to now as the warden of this prison system—must begin gathering his group of specially trained soldiers (thoughts). This special group of thoughts is a six-member group called the goon squad.

The goon squad is nothing but a group of specially trained prison guards that have been programmed to keep you in check—fearfully speaking! This six-member group consists of three officers, two sergeants, and one lieutenant whose names are as follow:

1. Officer Worry
2. Officer Scary
3. Officer Doubt
4. Sgt. Anxiety
5. Sgt. Stress
6. 1st Lieutenant Lie!

The most powerful, militant member of this entire group is 1st Lieutenant Lie. The rest of the crew heavily depends on his direction and leadership. 1st Lieutenant Lie is so filled with *lies* that not only does his name begin with it—it is the first three letters of his rank (lie-U-tenant).

1st Lieutenant Lie is the **first one to lie** and the first one to enforce the attack. Then he orders the rest of the crew to join in and compound this vicious attack on a continual basis. Your mind comes under intense attack and is at the mercy of these relentless and senseless group of thoughts 24-hours a day, 7 days a week!

The ultimate duty of 1st Lieutenant Lie is to keep a person's mind filled with lies but then he orders Sgt. Stress to monitor and compound this gruesome attack until the person keels over. I should forewarn you that anytime 1st Lieutenant Lie assigns Sgt. Anxiety and Sgt. Stress to monitor and compound an affect—he is *really* trying to knock you off (kill you!). It's only when he assigns Officer Worry, Officer Scary, and Officer Doubt that you know he only wants to torture you **subtly.** But when 1st lieutenant Lie assigns his two high-powered officers—Sgt. Anxiety and Sgt. Stress—oh, he has made the decision to **kill you violently!** He does not even want you as a prisoner any longer—for, he would much rather see you dead!

At this point, it looks like you are pretty much a done-deal unless you make a radical change to reverse this wrongful sentence and free yourself at once!

Now, because you are your own judge who God will base his judgment on—therefore, you must conduct your own court and rule against these hardened criminals in your life, i.e., fear, anxiety, stress, worry, scary, doubt, lie and others by imposing your sentence as you recite this decree:

"My Judgment Against Fear And His Staff:

Fear, I sentence you to death!
Anxiety, I sentence you to death!
Stress, I sentence you to death!
Doubt, I sentence you to death!
Worry, I sentence you to death!
Nervousness, I sentence you to death!
Intimidation, I sentence you to death!
Personal Lies, I sentence all of you to death!"

We are exalted or condemned by the words that we use. The Bible declares: *"Death and life are in the power of the tongue (Proverbs 18:21)."* So, let's condemn and sentence these accursed words of evil to death and speak the blessed words of righteousness—and truly live!

Chapter Thirteen

FEAR: The Eviction Notice!

Listen up! Listen up! I'm about to make my kingdom announcement by imposing evictions! So, when I call out your name, I want you to step forward and vacate my premises:

YOU: Fear!

FEAR: Yes.

YOU: You got to go!

FEAR: I'm sorry but I have no place else to go.

YOU: Well, I don't care where you go but you got to get the hell out of here!

YOU: Stress!

STRESS: Yes.

YOU: You got to go!

STRESS: I don't have any place else to go either.

YOU: Then go with Fear!

YOU: Anxiety, I ain't tryin' to hear it—you gotta to go!

ANXIETY: Very well.

YOU: Yeah, very well get out!

YOU: Next on my list is . . . Doubt!

DOUBT: Yeah, WHAT?

YOU: Yeah, WHAT? Did I hear you say . . . Yeah WHAT?

DOUBT: Yeah, WHAT?

YOU: Okay Mr. Smart Mouth, I never liked you anyway!

DOUBT: Well, the feelings are mutual.

YOU: Well I hope they are—just GET OUT! And tell the rest of your story walking and tell it outside my door! And all the rest of you freeloaders, families, relatives and friends of Fear—GET OUT OF MY HOUSE! **I HAVE AWAKENED** to the truth about your evils. All of you are nothing but noisy, lying, false-gossiping, deceiving and just all around BAD COMPANY!!! So, hurry up and get out because your beds have already been taken by a host of new and positive people (thoughts) who know how to treat a very good and expensive mansion (kingdom) with glory, honor, esteem and great respect!

So, all of ya'll GET OUT OF MY HOUSE and I hope that none of you have any place else to go— **YOU TROUBLEMAKERS!!!**

Chapter Fourteen

FEAR Is Charged In Universal Court!

STATE OF THE WORLD
Plaintiff

VS

FEAR
Defendant

Bailiff: All rise for the Honorable Universal Judge!

Judge: Please be seated! Let us begin our next case, indictment No. 06660, *Fear vs. The state of the world*. Fear may I ask you to please stand and state your full name.

Fear: Yes sir, your honor. My full name is:

False Evidence About Reality
First name

Falsely Envisioning Agonizing Results!
Last name

Judge: Defendant, do you want to be held in contempt of court for perjury?

Fear: No, sir your honor! But where did I perjure myself?

Judge: You have perjured by lying about your name! Sir, is not Fear your real name?

Fear: Yes sir, your honor!

Judge: So, why did you tell this court that your full name was false evidence about reality—falsely envisioning agonizing results?

Fear: Pardon me, your honor, I'm very sorry for this misunderstanding. Fear is what they call me for short.

Judge: Hmmm, I see! Well, let us proceed with the felony indictments that you have been universally charged with:

Count One, 1st Degree Murders!

Since the days of Adam and Eve, Fear alone has killed the same number of people that make up the total number currently on the planet, which tallies at six billion people. This means you are charged with six billion murders!

Judge: How do you plea?

Fear: Not guilty!

Judge: Count Two: **1st degree attempted murders!**

Since the days of Adam and Eve, Fear alone has caused enormous numbers of near-deaths calculated at one-half the number of *actual murders*. This means you are charged with three billion attempted murders!

Judge: How do you plea?

Fear: Not guilty!

Judge: Count Three: **1st degree suicides!**

Since the days of Adam and Eve, Fear alone has caused many people to be so mentally or emotionally stressed out that they were compelled to commit suicide by hanging themselves, or fatally shooting themselves, slitting their wrists, overdosing on lethal drugs or driving off road cliffs. These number of suicides are one half the numbers of *attempted murders*. This means you are charged with 1.5 billion suicides!

Judge: How do you plea?

Fear: Not guilty!

Judge: Count Four: **1st degree attempted suicides!**

Since the days of Adam and Eve, Fear alone has caused so many innocent people to be emotionally traumatized with deep depression that this caused them to make failed attempts at suicide either by failed strangulations, failed gun shot wounds, failed slit wrists and failed overdoses, etc. These number of attempted suicides are one half the numbers of actual suicides. This means you are charged with 750,000,000 million attempted suicides!

Judge: So, how do you plea?

Fear: Not guilty, your honor!

Judge: Let me ask you sir, how is it that in none of these cases are you guilty?

Fear: First, your honor, I didn't kill any of these people—all of these people killed or tried to kill themselves! I was merely marketing my company, i.e., *Fear & Associates*! We are a company that specializes in the promotional and marketing business of telling and selling false dreams, telling and selling false hopes; telling and selling illusions of pain, pressure, persecution and prosecution. We provide these services to all our clients and I might add that we do a damn good job of it! *Fear & Associates*, is a global group of skillfully trained and highly qualified professionals who have been in business since the beginning of man! Your honor, With All Due Respect To The Universal Court Of Life, if these people did not appreciate our services then it was within their rights and freedom to have gone elsewhere! *Fear & Associates* does not force people to believe our LIE—we merely and only suggest it! And by virtue of **free enterprise**—I have the God-Given right to offer my business to whoever seeks it!

Judge: Hmmm. I will make my final decision when I return from the judge's chamber. Court is now in recess!

One Minute Later

Bailiff: All rise for the Honorable Universal Judge, as the Judge will now render his decision.

Judge: You can all be seated. It is hereby the order of this court to set Fear **F-R-E-E** of all criminal charges. THIS COURT IS ADJOURNED!!!

The People: Wait a minute, wait a minute. This is an OUTRAGE! How is it that Fear is free of all criminal charges? This is a travesty of justice.

Conclusion: You Are Your Own Criminal Charged With Your Own Crime. Your Greatest Enemy Is That Very Familiar Person Who Is With You 24-hrs A Day: **You!**

Chapter Fifteen

The True Enemy

Enemy is *inner me*. It is this enemy which is the *inner me* that can bring about the en ê my (end-of-me). You don't have enemies; you only have *inner me* 's. It is *inner me* 's that are your enemies! Here's a short *inner me* Proverb:

> The *inner me*
> has always prevented me
> from reaching my goals.
> An outsider is not my enemy.
> For, I AM the only *inner me*
> that can bring about
> the en ê my (end-of-me).

YES, my greatest enemy is that neatly tucked away *inner me*! The *inner me* is my worst enemy. So, once I defeat my *inner me*—I have finally defeated my greatest enemy!

Inner me is the enemy that will bring about the en ê my (end-of-me).

-The End-
(But not <u>of me</u>!)

Chapter Sixteen

Fear: The Spiritual War Within!

"Put on the whole armour of God, that ye may be able to stand against the wiles (tricks) of the devil." – *Ephesians 6:11.*

The Bible said to put on the whole armor of God. God did not give us armor to go to an amusement park. God gave us armor to participate in WAR! We must be prepared to *spiritually* rumble!

As children of God, we are soldiers enlisted in his Spiritual Army. And if we are soldiers then we must be willing to fight. And if we are in a spiritual army, then there must be a spiritual war going on.

Spiritual means formless or invisible. There is an invisible war going on within every human soul whether you believe in the powers of God or not. This war didn't ask you: *"What is your religion?"* This war could care less whether you are a Baptist, Catholic, Protestant, Apostolic, Jehovah Witness, Mormon, Jewish, Muslim, Buddhist or Atheist. Your feelings about whether God exists or not will not stop or prevent the effects and impact of this type of war: **This spiritual war is within**.

So, are you ready to get involved? Are you prepared to engage? Are you willing to participate in this type of war? Quite frankly, this was not a multiple-choice question! This war doesn't require a show of hands. You are in this war whether you like the idea of war or not. This war is already in progress. Thus, Put On Your Armor And Prepare For Battle!

What type of battle is this? In the Bible, it describes the nature of this war in these words, *"For, we wrestle (battle) not against flesh and blood but against principalities, against powers, against the rulers of the darkness of this world, against spiritual wickedness in high places (Ephesians 6:12)."*

You may ask, what is *spiritual wickedness* in high places? Well, this scripture is talking about all the bad, evil, and wicked thoughts in the highest place known to man: **the human mind**. Even the sky above cannot surpass the heights of a man's mind. That is because a man's mind enabled him to surpass the sky when he invented the plane. A man's mind enabled him to surpass the sky when he made his trip to the moon. There is nothing in this universe that can surpass the height of a man's mind. Therefore, this *spiritual wickedness* in high places that the Bible is referring to, is none other than the human mind.

In the Bible, in the book of Isaiah, we are called *trees of righteousness (Isaiah 61:3)*. The Bible refers to us as trees and as trees we must stand against the wicked winds of the devil! The wicked winds of the devil are filled with a whirlwind of what the Bible refers to as *wiles*, which means tricks. The devil is Fear and Fear is trying to trick you! You are nothing but a spirit clothed in flesh. The devil or Fear is trying to trick your spirit (which is who you truly are) and that is the overall objective of this spiritual war within.

It is very important to point out that this spiritual war is an invisible war, which means that it cannot be seen by the naked eye. So, why is it called an **invisible** war? In the word invisible is "in" and "visible". The spirit woman and man are the only ones who can see this type of war. The physical eyes cannot see spiritual war—for, only a spirit can see the activities and transactions of a spiritual war! Your new pair of contact lens or glasses cannot illuminate this type of war. Again, this type of war is spiritual!

In order to be truly effective at this spiritual level of war—you will have to bring all your "**in's,**" not financial ends but spiritual "**in's,**" to the battlefield (mind). So, the first thing you must know are the fundamentals regarding the "**in's**" of life. Meaning, you are an *individual* and not an *out-dividual!* In the word "individual" are three words *in, divide, and dual* which means you are a dual or two-part being divided in two: There is a natural body and there is a spiritual body (1 Corinthians 15:44).

Next, you must have true *insight*. In the word "insight" are two words *in* and *sight*—which means, the more you go *in* the more you will get *sight*.

Next, you must allow *inspiration* to validate your intuition. Inside the word "inspiration" is *in* and *spire:* you have to go *in* before you can get *inspired!*

In the word "intuition" are three words *in tu it*, which means you must go *in to it* and not go *out from it.* Let's get ready for war, now that you know you "**in's**" of life. This brief little lesson will help you focus and become victorious against your greatest enemy!

In order to be victorious against this great enemy—we have to first be spiritually war-conscious! This was the reason why you had to first know your "in's" because this is an *inward* and *invisible* war. Therefore, we must always be conscious of this spiritual reality! So, what are the advantages of being spiritually war-conscious?

The first advantage is that you can identify with the **objective** of this war.

The second advantage of being spiritually war-conscious is that you can identify with **who the enemy is** and how to attack it.

The third advantage is that you can identify with all the invisible **weapons of war** used by the enemy, so that you can forge a defense and consequently prepare an attack.

However, if you're not spiritually war-conscious—first, you don't even believe that you are in a war (this is critical).

Second, you cannot identify that a war opponent even exists (this is fatal!).

Third, you don't even know how to defend yourself against these invisible weapons that are being used in this invisible war (this is suicidal).

Therefore, You Will Die Easily! You're just a sitting duck fighting in a blind war. You can't see those spiritual weapons but those weapons can see you clearly! You are like a wounded soldier without a paramedic and the end result is: You Will Bleed To Death.

Next, we must always know when we are on enemy territory. It is critical for a spiritual soldier to know when he or she is intruding on enemy territory. Thus, if a spiritual soldier is undergoing *Fear* then this soldier is in enemy territory.

If a spiritual soldier is operating in *doubt* then this soldier is in enemy territory. If a spiritual soldier is *worrying* about this and always *worrying* about that, then this soldier is within enemy territory; and if this same spiritual soldier is experiencing a strong sense of *anxiety* then this soldier is deep into enemy territory.

As a spiritual soldier of God's Spiritual Army—it is your duty to force *Fear, doubt, worry, nervousness, shyness, and anxiety* into captivity. *Fear, doubt, worry, nervousness, shyness and anxiety* should all be your personal POW's (prisoners of war).

Now, the thing you cannot let happen is in your attempt to place these POW's in captivity you let them place you inside instead. Well, not only would this be devastating if it should ever happen—but, also, it will be embarrassing!

Imagine this, on the physical realm. Let's say that you are a police officer escorting a prisoner to a cell and this prisoner "flips the script" and puts you in the cell instead! Well, not only will you probably lose your job—but also, you'll be the talk and laugh of the century!

On the spiritual realm, this happens over ninety percent of the time and it's nothing to laugh about at all! Truly, it is pathetic and embarrassing, yet it happens on a daily basis.

Again, your mind is the battlefield, where this spiritual war within is conducted. Your fierce enemies are the attributes of the devil i.e. *Fear, anxiety, stress, worry, doubt, nervousness, dislike, hatred, envy, jealousy, anger, resentment and lies.* These are just a few of the many attributes of the devil. Your enemy wears one of these satanic attributes—I guarantee you!

Strategy of War

The Apostle Paul executed, in my opinion, the most effective weapon in combating these spiritual POW's within by applying what is called **The Self-Crucifixion** method. The Apostle Paul said, *"I die daily. (1 Corinthians 15:31)."*

What Apostle Paul meant by that statement was not that he physically died and was physically resurrected then physically died again and was again physically resurrected. No, what Apostle Paul meant was that he put to death the old Paul: the old self; the old character, and the old thinking each and everyday.

Like Apostle Paul, **We Must Die Daily!** Every human being on this earth must die to our fleshly desires daily. We must each destroy the old self, the old attitude, the old character, the old thinking, the old ways, and the old actions. We must die daily! This simply means that we must have spiritual funeral services for our old thoughts and old way of thinking EVERYDAY!

We should have had a spiritual funeral service **yesterday, today** and schedule to have another one bright and early **tomorrow!** We should never run out of *self-funerals* until our old selves have completely vanished!

There are many men and women living today who have already accomplished this feat—so, it's very doable. Therefore, you can do it too!

I wish you Godspeed with the construction and development of your new self—as you establish your victory in the spiritual war within!

Chapter Seventeen

The Formula On Fear:
A stolen copy from off the desk of the devil

How to make human-fear?

Devil: It's my most masterful concoction and best-kept secret! First, you take something that is **False**. Next, you mix it and make it appear as if it is **Evidence** (truth). Then, you must go **About** making it this person's **Reality**. As a result, this person will begin *falsely* seeing or *envisioning* images of himself failing, hurting, or some other *agonizing* situation, which will ultimately bring about a very miserable and terrible *result*. This is my evil mixture, which promises to kill any soul. And if you properly inject this wicked formula into their minds according to my instructions—you will get a fear-component each and every time—I guarantee you! This is my official formula on *How To Make Human Fear*. So, I command you to: Be fruitful with this formula and multiply it! And if you do this properly, as I have commanded, ALL OF THEM will start dying off until eventually they are all dead. **This Is My Overall Objective!**

-A Confidential Document-

This is THE ANCIENT FORMULA OF FEAR stolen from the laboratory of Lucifer (Satan).

Shhh! Don't tell him I gave this to you!

Chapter Eighteen

FEAR:
The Five Things It Hates The Most

1. To be put last as if something else is more important!

2. To have someone planning, studying and plotting on how to defeat it!

3. To have someone grinning and smiling at it while it's chemically cooking its CRACK **to make you crack!**

4. To not be taken seriously!

5. And last but not least, FEAR hates it when You Act Like It Doesn't Exist! FEAR Hates This With A Passion!

Chapter Nineteen

FEAR:
The Thing That Turned A Child Into A Champ!

As a seven-year-old kid, like other seven-year-old kids, I deeply and religiously believed in the whole underground world of ghosts, haunted houses and haunted people. Yes, I was very terrified of the underground world yet I kept this all to myself. However, I noticed that all my friends shared this same fear of ghosts, haunted houses and all the rest of the haunted things, which came with it. There were many times when we would play around with the word "*haunted*" or "*the bogeyman*" in an effort to try to scare one another. For instance, if someone that we knew had unfortunately passed away—we would say such things like, "*Old man John is coming to haunt you!*" And although, we knew that the person who said it, had only done so, to make us afraid—we would all make a quick dash in fright anyway.

This whole thing about ghosts and haunted people coming back to life was something that I really didn't feel comfortable sharing with anyone— even my mother, especially being the big brother of a younger sister and brother. Even as a kid, I was always this tough guy—not a bully—but the duke of all my classes. Yet let you say, "*I hear a ghost,*"—I'd be the first one running!

Also, let me add, I was a little track star, which meant that I could run pretty fast. The ghost would have needed another *supporting* ghost to try to cut off my path, because believe me, I was truly fast!

So, as this young kid, I didn't want to discuss my fear of "*the darker world*" with anyone i.e., family, friends, relatives etc. Why? Because it appeared to me then, that I would be acting like a little sissy! So, you know, as the duke of my class—I couldn't *get down like that!* Hey, I had to be strong and just deal with it! So, I did exactly that for the next seven years.

Time passed and now I'm 14 years old. I'm still very much this rough and tough little kid! But, being a lot older, you could no longer scare me with the "*I hear a ghost*" drama anymore. I would look at you like you were crazy! But even though I was older, tougher, and a lot wiser—I still didn't have **an answer** to the question: "*Do you believe in the dark, underground world of spooks and spirits?*" Quite frankly, I still wouldn't have an answer to this question. Undoubtedly, my seven-year-old fear was not completely erased, and that was due to one simple reason—**I Never Truly Answered It!**

In school, they just don't teach you this stuff. Therefore, I thought that even if I'd asked the question to my teacher—she probably would have said that ghosts do not exist! Such a reply would have only taken every bit of just two seconds to say. However, this would have not been a good or helpful answer for me.

So, there I went more days, months and years with no answer to a seven-year-old fear. And it was not like I was really thinking about it everyday, either, because in all actuality I wasn't! Here I was in my prime and enjoying the fruits of youthfulness—I was having fun, I had myself a nice girlfriend, and we were having a ball!

Then all of a sudden, my life changed drastically in just one day, and the **unanswered** seven-year fear raised its ugly head like you wouldn't believe!

A Dreadful Night

On one of the worst evenings of my life, I came home to an empty house, and went directly to the bathroom. There I saw huge blotches of blood on the bathroom tiles and in the sink. Now my heart began racing because I was trying to figure who the blood belonged to. I quickly quit trying to figure it out because the fact was simply this: This blood is in my house and I Do Love everyone who lives in my house. So, this was no time to play doctor and perform a blood test or to try to put a face to that blood. It was just simple arithmetic for me:

> **Point one:** This blood is *in my house.*
> **Point two:** Everybody who lives in this
>   house—I love.
> **Point three:** No one who lives in this house
>   *is here.*

All of these calculations spelled: **We Have An Emergency Situation Here!!!**

It wasn't long before there was a knock on the door. It was our next-door neighbor; she told me that my mother, sister, and brother were all at the hospital because my uncle Joe had suffered a severe seizure.

The very sad news was that my uncle Joe had passed away from the trauma to his head. I'm not going to continue with the rest of the details of that painful day. But just know that we all loved our uncle Joe and may his beautiful spirit still live on through his beautiful daughter.

God wanted me to tell that real-life story because from it, I developed into a man: A Teenaged Man. My Uncle Joe did lived with us at that time, and he was like that older brother I never had. But after his passing something very strange and unexplained began happening to me the following day!

I began hearing noises from the bedroom where Uncle Joe had slept! It was actually the bed itself that was making a squeaking noise. I almost freaked out when I first heard it! Now, at that time, I watched a lot of television programs about other people claiming to have heard strange noises coming from revisited dead-relatives or ghosts etc. In any case, you would never think that this would one day happen to you.

Now, mind you, I never used drugs—so I couldn't understand why my mind was bugging out like this. Here I was, the average, normal fourteen-year-old kid who would have been the first kid to burst out laughing—with tears running down my face—if someone else had said that he or she had heard noises from a dead person. I would have looked at this person as if he (or she) was a Looney tune, but now I was this Looney tune! So I didn't feel comfortable about this at all!

For the most part, I had grown to be quite a courageous young man in spite of my seven year fear which by now I truly thought was completely behind me and gone forever. So I thought! As a fourteen-year-old kid, this really puzzled me because I no longer believed in ghosts or people coming back from the dead. So, I figured: *"If I didn't believe in it then how could I possibly still fear it?"*

The truth of the matter was that I had never really convinced my belief-system that ghosts or haunted things were not, in fact, true. I never really got my **answer** to this strange experience, which established this principle:

*"If you cannot explain something that's **eerie**, then it won't be much longer before it becomes **scary**. After EERIE comes SCARY."*

Because I couldn't explain this squeaking noise from the bed in which my uncle had once slept—I began to develop a fear each and every time I heard it! So, I agree with the above principle, "*If you cannot explain something that's **eerie**, then it won't be much longer before it becomes **scary**. After **EERIE** comes **SCARY!**"

However, there was something else that I thought was very strange. These bed-squeaking noises would only happen when I was home alone! Hmmm, I thought this was very odd and weird! For instance, if any one of my relatives were in the house with me, the noises wouldn't happen. It was only when I was alone that I would hear these noises.

At this point, I really thought I was flipping out! So to prevent myself from hearing these noises, I would only come home when I knew someone else would be there.

There were times when I would come home and begin watching TV and then the question would dawn on me that: "*Hey, you do know that you're here by yourself?*" And lo, and behold, the bed-squeaking noises would begin! And I would quietly get up and be out the door. By the way, I'd put up with this unexplained fear for a couple of months. I mean, I just kept running from this fear. And every time I would hear those bed-squeaking noises—**I'd be like Houdini**, I was magically out the door!

This fear really wore me out! I was getting tired of fearing this thing. I couldn't understand how I could be this tough guy outside the house and such a sissy within it! This was the thing I just couldn't understand and it began to emotionally plague me. Ultimately, came the unforgettable day that changed my life forever—I still remember it like it was yesterday.

The Big Showdown!

I came home worn-out and fresh off a very heated argument with my, then, girlfriend. I sat there in the living room tired and frustrated with how horrible my day had turned out to be. I think I'd sat in the house, for about three hours—yet still angry and mad. Then out of nowhere came the thought: *"Are you aware that you are here by yourself?"* And right after that question I heard those bed-squeaking noises. But, this was the wrong day. I was tired, angry, and frustrated all at the same time and was not leaving the house for anything, whether aliens, ghosts or the five-headed monsters from outer space! These were the thoughts that were running through my head: "*I'm tired; I'm mad; I'm angry; I'm frustrated and I'm NOT trying to hear this ghost stuff today! This is the wrong day and wrong dude!*"

So, like a bat out of hell, I transformed into a **WILD, CRAZED MANIAC** and began storming into the bedroom where the noises were and began hollering and screaming, "*What's up, so you want to talk? Let's talk!!! I'm tired of running out this house! Let's be men and talk like men!!! The worst thing you can do to me is kill me. Well, I'm not afraid of death! So, let's talk. So, what's up?*" And miraculously the noises just mysteriously stopped! I mean the bedroom and the entire atmosphere became utterly silent. I was numbed and stunned almost in sheer disbelief.

And since that day, I'm proud to say that I have never heard those noises ever again! I really got a little upset with myself because that was all I had to do in the first place. I had to come **face-to-face** with that which I secretly feared the most! So, when I finally did that—fear just disappeared! It vanished and evaporated like the LIE that it was and is. It was almost like it really wanted me to take that bold approach, but I knew better than that!

The bondage of fear had to release me. Not because it wanted to parole me *for being on good behavior*—but because, I had violently broken lose! Fear had no other choice but to let me go free because once I broke the chains—**I was already set free!** The shackles that bound me were all shattered into pieces! When you finally break loose from the chains of Fear, you are a free WOMAN— you are a free MAN.

I'd unfastened those psychological handcuffs by violently breaking them loose! When I finally broke loose from my childhood fear—I became a free spirit.

Although, just 14 years old and still relatively new to life—I felt liberated. I felt as though I had captured a **brand new life** when I'd finally freed myself from a horrible life of living in fear.

The sky looked different; the trees, the street corners and the street signs, they all looked different. My school, both inside and outside, looked different. My classmates seemed to me to have a different glare to their eyes. The house where I lived and everything in it—even the very bedroom where the noises *appeared* to have been coming from, looked different. I was so bold with my **new, found life** and self-released from the prison of Fear—that I even went as far as sleeping in the very bedroom where all the squeaking noises went down. And I might add that I slept very good that night. I felt awesome; I felt beautiful; I felt FREE!!!

False Evidence About Reality

You will never really start living until you finally stop fearing!

It was only when I finally broke my chains and escaped the bondage of Fear that I knew Fear was all a bluff and nothing but *False Evidence About Reality*. When something is real, it cannot be changed! When something is real—its realness does not waver just because you are mad or angry on a particular day. Do you think the laws of righteousness will waver or change its program just because you might be angry or mad on a particular day? Of course not! Why is this? It is because the laws of righteousness are constant, consistent, and correct. The only laws that waver under pressure are false laws and/or laws that are not real. And make no mistake about it—I'm talking about the laws of Fear.

Fear is *False Evidence About Reality*; Fear is the biggest bluffer in the world. Fear abides by a law that is fake by nature, phony by profession, and false and unreal by purpose of design. Fear governs off a baseless foundation. As soon as I had put pressure on it to prove its claim—**It Ran!** Fear appeared to have *feared* me and I haven't seen that type of FEAR in my life ever since!

All of this taught me a valuable lesson: You have to take Fear to the max and once you do that—it will fold its cards! Why? Because Fear knows, it doesn't have a winning hand. Here is the overall conclusion:

You Can Drive Yourself Crazy!

The mind is a beautiful thing yet at the same time—it can be functionally psychotic. Yet the whole thing about this GHOST dynamic is that it is absolutely real IF YOU THINK IT IS! But it's not *real* outside of that.

"A ghost is only a ghost to the host—NO HOST; NO GHOST. It's just that simple!"

I mean just think: If something is real then it should ring true no matter what. For example, if there are five people in a room and out of this group of five—you are the only one that is strangely hearing loud, ghostly noises then—YOU MAY BE A MENTAL DING DONG!!!

If something is universally true and real—it will manifest its truthfulness and realness no matter who is in the room. Since the other people in the room could not hear those LOUD noises (which you and you alone claimed to have heard)— this proves that there is something going on in your mind. When your mind is going through this type of experience—this is the result of a morbid misunderstanding about life, which must be corrected. And the only way to finally get this fixed is by finding an answer, which says: "Those noises didn't actually exist!"

When something actually exists this means **the natural laws of life works for you like it works for everybody else.** So, if you and four other people are all sitting down together and watching television then this means that all five of you should be getting the same AUDIO and VISUAL. But if you were to abruptly jump up and begin screaming that you heard and saw a ghost next to the TV and the other four people in the room did not hear or see this alleged ghost then this means that they did not get the same AUDIO and VISUAL that you did. This leads to one conclusion: This Is Not An Actual or Universal Fact. Therefore, this strange phenomenon did not actually exist because this law did not work for the other people in the room as it had worked for you! And this is the very problem that I have with people who have claimed to have heard noises *coming from the dead.*

What I always found ironic is that cats and dogs are creatures too. Yet we never hear any reports of someone being haunted by the spirit of a dead dog barking or the spirit of a dead cat meowing. I find this interesting!

So back to the point, **"A ghost is only a ghost to the host—NO HOST; NO GHOST. It's just that simple!"** If something is really and actually occurring then I and whoever else in the same vicinity should be able to bear-witness and attest to this fact as well. If no one except the person who made the claim can attest to this so-called fact—it proves that it is only a mirage, an illusion and an absolute farce.

Empowerment Time!

It's very important that we *train the brain to reign!* Fear is a merciless, ruthless, and senseless demon, which will seek to destroy everyone, even children. Fear has no emotion, sympathy, or empathy for age—the only criteria for Fear is for it to have a mind to dwell in, and the next stop is straight to hell!

So, I implore parents to pay very close attention to your child or children and try to talk to them about the things they are uncertain about! I purposely chose the words "*uncertain about*" as opposed to saying *Fear*, because this generation is not much different from my generation. Meaning, they think they're tough, little adults or know-it-all little people. They are not going to come right out and tell you all *the things that they Fear*. So, ask them about the root of Fear, which is **uncertainty** and the **unknown**. Fear is born out of the underground world of the unknown.

When one's knowledge cannot explain why something is occurring—this makes a perfect, breeding ground for the formation of FEAR.

So, start asking your children questions like: *What is your idea or opinion about life or what is your idea or opinion about death?* These are two powerful little questions that can open up for you a whole new perspective of the state of your child's thoughts about how he or she sees life, or doesn't see it!

Such a conversational exchange may even open up a Pandora box which may consist of strange demons or Fears of all kinds. Quite frankly, this is the mental area where you would want to be.

Truly, it is in this department of Fear where the child is going to need big time assistance from mommy and/or daddy—because as I've mentioned in a previous chapter—**Fear Doesn't Play; Fear Kills.**

So, please, parents help your children in combating this demon called Fear. Fear's ultimate goal is to steal, kill, and destroy anyone it can devour: **This Includes Children!**

Fear kills indiscriminately! There is a long list of children who have been killed by Fear. So, let this NOT happen to your child or children. Take Action Now!

Fear is just as dangerous, powerful, and poisonous for a child as it is for an adult!

Parents, there is no such thing as "fear junior," "fear III," or "fear 4 kidz"! There are no child-sized versions of Fear because there is only one Fear—and it is always spelled with a capital "F". This demon called Fear fits all sizes, i.e., toddlers, small children, big children, teenagers, adults, and the elderly.

The Bogeyman

We as parents love using this ancient parental tool—the imaginary bogeyman. However, it is a feeble attempt to bring the child into submission after all other tactics have miserably failed. Thus, the parent is saying: *"I can't seem to control you (little boy)—so I MUST sic the devil on you!"*

The bogeyman is nothing but Fear. And Fear is nothing but the devil. Parents, how dare you sic the devil on your children. Parents should not have to fabricate a hoax just to bring their children into submission.

Establish your words as Lord, King and The Law of The Land. As parents, we must stop depending on the evil effects of this imaginary thing called the bogeyman. Get respect from your children by the strength of your name and not by the name of a made-up bogeyman.

Furthermore, if you make a habit of using the bogeyman—the child will grow to never listen to you but only listen to the call of the bogeyman. For a parent, this is the worst disciplinary relationship to have with your child—as the child never learns to respect the command of your voice.

Fear loves it when parents play these silly games or when they do not take him seriously. In so doing, Fear is given the freedom to continue to emotionally *molest* their children. Parents are very protective against sexual molestation yet they let their guards down totally against the very serious, emotional child-molester called Fear.

Personally, I would never allow my children to watch horror movies. I'm not going to help develop an evil baby in them called Fear. What may now seem as harmless or just fun and entertainment will soon grow to be an adult nightmare! **You can't play with Fear; Fear will kill you!** Fear will kill you and won't think two seconds about your burial! Even at your funeral, Fear won't care about how many people are crying and how many will be missing you so dearly. Fear is careless, merciless and ruthless.

Fear Is Fearless

Fear doesn't *fear* anything and that is one of the main reasons why Fear is so powerfully effective. Fear knows that the chemical composition of FEAR will paralyze you and will eventually shut you down completely!

Fear knows that if it were to personally *fear* this would ultimately shut down its entire operation. Fear would be out of business and wouldn't be able to get to you and the rest of the people around the world. You've heard the old saying before, "*You can't take your own medicine.*" Well, this describes Fear perfectly. Fear knows that it cannot take its own medicine because what Fear has is NOT MEDICINE, but a poison!

Once you get into a habit of consistently dosing yourself with this type of poison—it won't be long before you will drop flat dead! Again, you can't play with Fear; Fear will kill you! There is but one thing certain about something you *fear*—it is knowing that if you don't manage to get an answer for it soon—it will come to revisit you at a time in your life, which will be the worst time of your life— **And It Will Rip You To Pieces!**

So, I recommend that you get an answer to whatever it is that you *fear*—right now, while you are at your strongest. Or else, you will have to come up with an answer when you are truly at your weakest! Now, to our next chapter entitled...

Chapter Twenty

The Four Departments of FEAR

(1) Foresight: what you *see* as in false visions.

(2) Emotions: what you *feel* as in false feelings.

(3) Audio: what you *hear* as in listening to lies.

(4) Ration: what you *rationalize* as in discerning. Meaning, once you start to *discern*—Fear will become a *concern*.

Discernment is the original birthplace and marks the birth date of Human Fear.

The Ration Factor is the *golden key* for eliminating human fear. Meaning, if you cut off rationalizing—you could never Fear!

Fear needs you to rationalize or *analyze, calculate and estimate* it in order for it to be effective. If you refuse to **calculate** Fear—it cannot **annihilate!**

The moment you refuse to *analyze, calculate and estimate* a fearful situation—Fear will be forced to a stalemate! Fear will not be able to move—so it will be impossible for it to be able to move YOU! So, don't *calculate it* or *estimate it* and you can never be *annihilated by it!*

Chapter Twenty-One

The Fear of The Lord

The Bible says, *"The fear of the LORD is the beginning of knowledge."* But the Bible also says, *"For God hath not put in us the spirit of fear (2 Timothy 1:7).* Now, is God contradicting himself? Absolutely not! This is just a case of some careless theologians mishandling the scriptures of God (WARNING!):

"For, I testify unto every man that heareth the words of the prophecy of this book, if any man shall add unto these things, God shall add unto him the plagues that are written in this book:

And if any man shall take away from the words of the book of this prophecy, God shall take away from his part out of the book of life and out of the holy city and from the things which are written in this book (Revelations 22:18-19)."

Thousands of years ago, The Most High God foresaw these spiritual knuckleheads (who refer to themselves as theologians) messing up this Old Testament Scripture! Thus, God preserved a great scripture on this matter in the New Testament, which left no stones unturned: *"God is love; and he that dwelleth in love dwelleth in God, and God in him"* (1 John 4:16).

Biblically, I have yet to find where God said: *"God is fear and he that dwelleth in fear dwelleth in God and God in him."* That cannot be found in the Bible.

God is Love and his spiritual children are lovers. God has NOT put the spirit of Fear in us. Why did God choose not to instill the spirit of fear in us? Well, if God had put the spirit of Fear in us, this would have totally violated his first commandment, which reads: *"Thou shalt have no other gods before me"* (Exodus 20:3). Fear is this evil thing, which puts another god before GOD.

God is Love—the righteous God.
Fear is the devil—the evil god.

Love and *Fear* are acts of serving. *Love* is a service. *Fear* is a service. We cannot *love* and *fear* the same God at the same time. This is what the Bible defines as **serving two masters!** In the book of Matthew it reads: *"No man can serve two masters: for either he will hate the one and love the other, or else* he will hold to one and despise the other *(Matthew 6:24).*

In the book of Exodus, it reads: *"For, I the Lord, thy God am a jealous God (Exodus 20:5)."* We are prohibited from serving two masters because the God that we serve is a jealous God.

God is *Love* and God doesn't want us to *fear* him when there are so many reasons to *love* him. God doesn't get any kicks out of pumping *fear* into us; God is only concerned with pumping *love* into us. We are not meant to be "*God-fearing people.*" When a person says: *"I'm a God-fearing man of God "*—this person is actually saying: *"I'm a God-devilish man of God."* Truly, you will go straight to hell talking like that and quickly!

On the contrary, we are created and meant to be *God-loving* people. We're not supposed to *fear* God—we're supposed to *love* him.

Remember, Fear is just the devil going by a different name! The meaning of fear has not changed from our previous chapters and its meaning is not changing in this one. Fear is the devil and there is no changing this reality whatsoever!

The term "*God-fearing*" is abominable—yet more than that—it is extremely blasphemous!

People can choose to do their little hyphening with "*God-fearing*" if they want, which has become very trendy with a lot of religious folks. But in the eyes of God—this is blasphemous! How dare these people associate an evil god with God **in the name of a hyphen and especially IN THE NAME OF JESUS!** This is a primary reason why over 90% of all churches are so screwed up to this day. This comes because all of them are religiously practicing and saying the same things.

Do you think that in the term *God-fearing*, the **hyphen** (-) next to God, is spiritually acceptable? This hyphen is going to send you to an early spiritual grave. I implore you to ask God for forgiveness and immediately abandon this spiritual malpractice at once.

The term *God-fearing* is spiritually unhealthy, dangerous, and abominable in the eyes of God. Yet having "love" as a hyphen next to God (as in *God-loving*) is a proper and an acceptable term; and its usage has already been biblically approved!

God is Love and fear is the devil. So, when people associate or bring together God and the devil (fear) to make a word, this is by far the worst sinful combination. It just does not spiritually mix!

Associating fear with God—as in the term, *God-fearing*, is like an electrical negative cable trying to defy the laws of mixing together with a positive cable—the only result is electrocution! Therefore, when a person says: *"I'm a God-fearing person"* —this is **spiritual electrocution!** This is the old electric chair being applied on the spiritual realm.

We will never be able to get to heaven talking like this. The book of Proverbs says: *"Thou are snared (entrapped) with the words of thy mouth (6:2)."*

In the Bible, the first book of John chapter 4:16, it reads: *"There is no fear in love, but perfect love casteth out fear because fear hath torment (great pain)."*

It is **Perfect Love** that casts out fear and such love does not align itself with fear. He that feareth is not made perfect in love. So, as children of God, we need to cast out *fearing* from God, because this prevents Perfect Love (Agape).

God said: *"Fear not me* (Malachi 3:5)." For, God is not in the *FEAR BUSINESS*—it is the devil who runs this department! The devil is the founder and chairman of all fears. Fear is not a product that God can use "in" his kingdom. Fear is just the product that God uses to prepare us "for" his kingdom.

Again, God did not put in us the *spirit of fear*—we only have time to love HIM. *God-fearing* is a term for the confused child. *God-loving* is Perfect Love for the child of perfect understanding!

Thus, we have no time to fear THE LORD because all this time can be best spent LOVING HIM!

Chapter Twenty-Two

THE LIE
Broken Down To The Fear*est* Degree!

The spiritual power called a LIE is an internal enemy that spends the entire day in your mind and rests the entire night marinating in your soul. The evil power called a LIE is an enemy. LIE lied about God, His righteousness, His truth and His enemies when he (LIE) is one of those enemies. The Bible says, "*Let God arise (in your spirit), let his enemies be scattered; let also that hate him flee before him. As smoke is driven away, so drive them away (Psalms 68:1-2).*"

Truly, a LIE can be driven away like smoke because that's exactly what a LIE is—meaning, it's an evaporated *form of smoke!* A LIE means Language In Evaporation!

A language is a *group of words*; a group of words are called *thoughts*; thoughts are called *spirits*; *you are a spirit*; and you are *your greatest enemy.* So, the LIE is the enemy, which exists inside of you and *it must be driven away!*

As smoke is driven away, so drive them (lies) away.

A LIE is an evaporated language because it has no substance to keep it solidified or alive. Consequently, it has to vanish or evaporate in midair like smoke. God's Power is Spirit *with substance*—so it lasts eternally and forever. The devil's power is spirit *without substance*—so it vanishes and evaporates like smoke! This is the life and death of a LIE and it all happens very quickly.

A LIE has the shortest life span of all things in creation. The natural life of a LIE can only last *a few seconds* then it must die or evaporate like smoke! What the devil simply does is suggest this evaporated language, which he knows will only last for *a few seconds* before it evaporates in your mind. Yet he hopes that it will catch your interest beyond this point. And he hopes that you will begin hammering these *vanishing words* within the fabric of your soul and thereby, keep the evaporated words alive.

When the devil has successfully accomplished this within your soul—you have given birth to the devil's demonic baby, which he named a LIE. So, what was once a Language In Evaporation has now become a Language In Existence or intrinsically existing in you! Yes, you have backslid or switched over to the other side and have privately formed an intimate marriage with your number one archenemy by secretly having his evil and demonic child called a LIE. The evil business once called "*Fear & Associates*"—now, reads: "*Fear, Associates and You.*"

Fear, Associates and You are promulgating voodoo!

The deadly tobacco smoke and the deadly LIE have the same life span—*just a few seconds!* A LIE should not last beyond *a few seconds*. And if it is still alive after that—it's no longer the natural effects of the LIE—it's YOU!

When a LIE or an evaporated language lasts longer than *a few seconds* this means that the devil just hired you and gave you a job! If you allow it to live longer, it means that you are filling out the devil's application not even realizing that you already have the job!

The devil is the founder and chairman of *Fear & Associates*, which only sells one exclusive product—an evaporated language properly called a LIE. This is the only product that the devil sells exclusively and he (the devil) has the patent and authority to sell it to whoever regardless of sex, age, race, color, class or creed.

Moreover, the devil is not required to inform us about the expiration or life expectancy of his product. As God has already informed us of this. God clearly stated that the life expectancy of a LIE is as that of smoke: "*As smoke is driven away, so drive them (lies) away.*"

A LIE should not last beyond a few seconds! However, many people have carried lies for days, weeks, months, years, and sometimes even decades!

A LIE should never go beyond *a few seconds* because anything beyond that point means that those words have been saved, **born again** and have received personal salvation from you. The LIE will continue to seek and pursue your spiritual demise, until it leads to a physical one! Well, that's just the evil nature of a LIE, which says:

(1) **Save me!**
(2) **Thank you!**
(3) **But now, I must continue my mission to DESTROY YOU!**

Truly, it's nothing personal with a LIE. It's just the very nature of its assignment.

The LIE is the only product that Fear uses to deceive the world. Everything else is only a variation of this same LIE just told in a different way, a different style and with a different affect but ultimately achieving the same identical result: **Deception then Destruction!**

In the word "Fear" is the word "**ear**". So, before you can **Fear it**–you must first **hear it!** And the only way it can be heard is through its language–this fading, withering and evaporated language called nothing but a LIE.

Thus, beware of these evaporated languages, which are nothing but evaporated lies because anything lasting longer than *a few seconds* means You're Filling Out An Application And Working For The Devil!

THIS IS: The LIE Broken Down To The Fear*est* Degree!

Chapter Twenty-Three

Fear and The Magnetic Job-Effect!

In the Bible, the Book of Job is a great and inspirational story that serves as a remarkable representation of true faith in God. However, the Bible is not a book that reveals scriptures so that they only make sense or have relevance to those who make up the script!

On the contrary, most scriptures make the most sense one to two thousand years later, or well after the script have already been written. Most scriptures have a more profound meaning for other generations of people rather than the people the stories were originally written about. This brings us to the very interesting story of Job.

The Book of Job was divinely meant to be more than just a story in Job's day and time—but more of a global teaching for the world in this day and time!

Job's Greatest Fear

The Bible describes Job's Fear in the areas of his personal life, health, family, and business.

However, the highlight of Job's spiritual escapade rests with his most famous quote: "*For the thing which I greatly feared is come upon me (Job 3:25).*" The most important piece to this very popular biblical quotation is one principle: **Fear Is A Magnet.**

All thoughts are *magnetic,* and Fear has one of the strongest *magnetic influences* of all human thoughts. For the most part, we should not be surprised to learn that **thoughts are magnetic!**

We live in a gigantic *magnetic* field called the universe. The universe is nothing but a huge *field of magnets* i.e., planets, poles, plants, power, and people.

If you are a member of the human race, then *you are a magnet.* You cannot exist in this universe and be otherwise. So, if you are not a *magnet* then you are NOT from here—you are a part of another universe, which I know nothing about!

The universe is a *magnetic field* and the power that electrically charges all *magnets in the universe.* What manner of power do you think keeps you charged each and everyday? Are you plugged into an electrical socket on a wall? Of course, you're not. So, what physically charges your body's cellular batteries and allows you to perform your physical activities and movements?

The average working man expends a lot of electrical or magnetic energy up until he decides to end his day and get rest. What is rest? The word *rest* comes from the latin word *restaurare*, which means to renew, rebuild or restore. Man seeks to be restored, recharged, and re-energized each and everyday. Well, the only thing that can re-supply man's cellular batteries is within this magnetic field of the universe.

Scientists agree that humans are magnets. William H. Philpott, MD, one of the leading scientists in the field of electromagnetism, says: "*It is fundamental that we understand that man is an electromagnetic organism! Electricity flows through human nerves the same as electricity flows through electric wires.*" In India, a group of scientists had this to say: "*Every single cell in the body is an electrical unit and has a magnetic field of its own.*" My point exactly—**You Are A Magnet!**

Magnetic Man and Thoughts

The things that you *do*, you do them magnetically. The people that you *attract*, you attract magnetically. The *thoughts* that you think, you think them magnetically. Again, You Are A Magnet! Yet the Bible says: "*For as he thinketh in his heart, so is he (Proverbs 23:7).*"

Well, if this is true then let's do a little deductive reasoning:

(a) If a *magnet* equals you (Magnet = You)
(b) And if *You* equals thought (You = Thought)
(c) Then, *Thought* equals magnet (Thought = Magnet).

This is known as a syllogism and it says, "*If a=b and b=c then a=c.*" Is that not what we were taught about syllogisms?

Now that it is proven that thoughts are magnetic—we should have no problem realizing what truly happened with our good brother Job. Job said: "*For, the thing which I greatly feared is come (or magnetized) upon me.*" This is the biblical lesson that every believing man, woman, and child of God must take from the beautifully told story of Job.

We must truly understand that **Fear Is A Magnet!** We will always attract and draw to us what we openly or secretly fear. So, whatever we openly or secretly fear will become *our personal magnet*. Whatever we openly and secretly fear, it will always seem to follow us and know how to find us no matter where we are or what we are doing. This is officially called **The Magnetic Job-Effect!**

The Magnetic Job-Effect simply means whatever you FEAR will APPEAR! Thus, if you don't want something to *appear* then don't *fear* it! Fear is a magnet and a very powerful one at that!

The Heart-Barometer

The heart-barometer is a personal Lie detector (polygraph system). The heart knows when you are in fear and it knows if you are still being affected by fear's lie.

There are people who are skilled in how to beat *technology's polygraph system* but no one can beat or fool the *human polygraph system* called the heart.

The heart knows when you are not being truthful or true to your words. Meaning, if you're telling yourself that you do not fear something, but your heart is beating to a whole other tune—then this means that the heart is not buying or accepting your conviction on this matter at all. **This means that you have to make a physiological adjustment and quickly!**

In order to make this physiological adjustment so the heart will be able to respond positively—you must change your thought-pattern.

Obviously, your thought-pattern is *out of whack* or out of line with all the things that you've supposedly learned about Fear.

However, once you have re-established that Fear is merely a false conviction and an evaporated lie—you will then begin to notice the rhythm of your heart beating to a consenting tune attesting you have re-established your conviction.

The heart-barometer is a very important way to monitor your control of Fear or lack thereof. It gives you an indication of how firmly and deeply rooted your faith is in a particular situation— namely, if it is attacked by Fear. If applied effectively, **the heart-barometer** will forecast all of Fear's spiritually severe thunderstorms—especially the earthquake force of the *magnetic Job-effect!*

The magnetic Job-effect truly says: "Whatever you FEAR will APPEAR." The heart-barometer's role is to keep you aware of the magnetic Job-effect by detecting your level of Fear according to the rate of *heart-bpms* (beats per minute).

The heart-barometer principle says that the harder the heart throbs in Fear—the stronger the magnet in Fear pulls! **I repeat, the harder the heart throbs in Fear—the stronger the magnet in Fear pulls!** So, it's very important to monitor your heart's *bpms* because the harder and quicker the heart beats in Fear the stronger and faster the magnet in Fear will pull this very thing into fruition (existence!).

However, this same magnetism of thought also works in reverse. Meaning, if there is a negative magnet that can draw things to it—then there has to be a contrary or opposing force, which can do the same thing in reverse. And this powerful opposing force to the negative magnet is none other than the wonderful magnet of positivity.

The Positive Magnet

Positivity or the positive magnet is one's belief and faith in the system of God's Universal Laws of Righteousness. Therefore, if your belief-system is based on righteousness then it serves as a positive magnet and will produce a magnetism of its own kind.

The heart barometer principle will help you determine the extent of your belief-system. It can measure the extent of your backsliding in the faith department. Yes, your heart does more than pumping your daily 2,000 gallons of blood. The Bible clearly points out that the heart serves another purpose: *"For as he thinketh (believe) in his heart, so is he."*

So, you are what you believe. And if you DO NOT believe in anything—you *spiritually* don't exist! However, it is only the things you truly believe, which will bring you a certain kind of magnetism, whether positive or negative.

Your thoughts will establish their manner of magnetism. They will draw the very nature of their own kind based on what you truly, clearly and sincerely believe!

The Power of Believing

The Magnetic Job-Effect will produce a Fear-Magnet, which will cause those things that we fear to appear! But how do we counter-attack or de-magnetize this negative effect? It is by trusting in the **Power of Believing**.

What is trusting in the **Power of Believing?** It is knowing that once you start believing in a particular thing something miraculous will immediately begin taking place in your mind. These thoughts will affect the hormonal activity of your brain, which will produce changes in the chemistry of your body. Your body becomes a magnetic field of chemistry. And lo and behold, you will start attracting things and situations by the very nature of your thoughts according to its kind!

As he thinketh in his heart, so is he. As she thinketh in her heart, so is she.

Parental Power

In many languages around the world, parents warn their children, "*Stay away from negative people because they will draw nothing but trouble.*" For centuries, parents have instinctively discovered—as unofficial, true human-electromagnetic scientists—the magnetic effect of human behaviors.

Parents discovered this seemingly complex concept, long before it was given its scientific name. Yet what parents have failed to realize was that the power of Fear works the exact same way.

Fear is this terribly evil **bad-boy**, this cruel, mean and crazy Fifth wheel! Mommy and daddy have warned us about staying away from negative boys and girls in the neighborhood and even at school. Yet mommy and daddy didn't warn us about staying away from this *other* evil boy who is everywhere. Yeah, this *other* evil boy is constantly robbing, stealing, scandalizing, assaulting, and brutally killing innocent men, women, and children for sheer entertainment! This cruel, bad, mean and evil boy's name is *False Evidence About Reality–Falsely Envisioning Agonizing Results* but they call him FEAR for short!

Fear: The Annoying Co-worker

Fear is that *co-worker* at your job. Specifically, Fear is working through the mind of this co-worker, this annoying *co-worker* that gets on your nerves and literally drives you crazy. Fear, through the mind of the *co-worker*, is always meddling in your personal affairs and never wants to see you get ahead. Fear, through the mind of the *co-worker*, never has anything positive to say—I MEAN NEVER! If you were to say, "I think I will ask for a promotion"—Fear, through the mind of the *co-worker*, will say: *"You're not going to get it, so don't waste your time!"*

If you were to say: "I think I'll ask for a pay raise." Fear, through the mind of the *co-worker*, will say: *"You are going to be so embarrassed and depressed when the boss says no."* And if you were to say: "I'm thinking about giving up this job for a much better job where I can make some real progress in my life." Fear, through the mind of the *co-worker*, will say: *"But what if it doesn't work out? Although this may not be the best job for you and it probably doesn't have the best group of people. But it's still a job. And at least you know what you are getting. However, with another job you don't really know what you will be getting. So, you just need to stay where you are!"* This is the poisonous effect of Fear.

If you fear making progress then you will NOT make any progress because *whatsoever you fear will appear.* **This Is The Magnetic Job-Effect!**

The magnetic Job-effect says: "*If you fear improving your life-situation due to fear of failure then failure will become the very thing that you will magnetize in your life.*" Fear is this negative magnetic thought that sits in your mind and begins its work of attracting all those things that you fear more closely to you. Fear is a magnet and a negative magnet at that!

Fear: The Abusive Relationship

Fear lives in that physically and emotionally abusive relationship that says: "*If I were to end this relationship right now, my life will then be back to being boring. And I will go back to being lonely, depressed and will eventually have to go back to that whole dating-scene all over again.*"

It also lives in that physically and emotionally abusive relationship that says: "*If I were to leave this abusive relationship then all my family and friends will feverishly gloat and say the horrible words: I TOLD YOU SO! I told you that he was no good for you and that the two of you would never work out, but you didn't want to listen to me.*"

Fear is in that physically and emotionally abusive relationship that says: "*If I were to report this physical assault and abuse to the proper authorities or if I should decide to leave him finally and for good–I believe he will really try to KILL ME.*" However, the unfortunate news is that there are countless cases where women, in very physically abusive relationships, have feared death so much that they unfortunately magnetized their own demise. Fear is a magnet and a negative magnet at that!

Fear and the Sexual Abuser

Fear is in that sexually abusive relationship of incest where your close relative (father, uncle, brother, or cousin) is secretly having or has had sex with you, but you are afraid to mention it to anyone because it may be publicized in the newspapers then almost the whole world will be exposed to your personal business i.e., neighbors, friends, other relatives and even all the people at your school.

Fear is also in that same sexually abusive relationship of incest, but you are afraid to mention it to your mother because she's not going to believe you anyway. She's going to think that you are only making this up because you're just looking for attention or because you're just trying to destroy the family, her marriage or the relationship with her boyfriend.

And Fear is in that same sexually abusive relationship of incest, but you are afraid to mention it to anyone because if you were to tell someone, the victimizer has said that he would badly hurt you and beat you miserably. **Yet that which you fear is appearing anyway.** For, he is already hurting you terribly through your intense Fear. What you feared has already appeared. Fear is a magnet and a negative magnet at that!

So, please understand the power of Fear and its magnetic abilities to draw evil, negative, and unpleasant things in your life. Job found this out in the worst way. And it was from Job's life experiences with Fear that *The Magnetic Job-Effect* was born. So, re-read this very important chapter again and again. And be sure to diligently study and practice the **heart-barometer principle**, as this will enable you to detect the powerful affects of *The Magnetic Job-Effect.*

Chapter Twenty-Four

Laughter Kills The First Few Stages of FEAR

Laughter produces hormonal chemicals that can kill the most powerful, hormonal chemicals produced by the human Fear. **It's all a chemical combat!** Thus, whichever has the most chemical secretions wins the battle of controlling this person's mind for that particular moment or until the effects of the chemical wears off!

This is how it works: Let's say you have just opened your mail to find a cancellation, an eviction, or repossession notice—the first thing you must IMMEDIATELY do is **laugh at it!**

"*The righteous also shall see, and FEAR, and shall laugh at him.*" —*Psalms 52:6.*

Here's what you've just done: You have created a chemical that will immediately douse the beginning stages of Fear. Just as a road is most slippery in the first few minutes of rainfall—so to Fear is the most tricky, slippery, and hazardous in the first few minutes of its storm. Therefore, you must douse the first few flames of Fear *fast* because these are the deadliest!

It's only right that I inform you that laughter is not going to stop FEAR dead in its tracks, just that quickly. No, it's not suppose to! The thing you want to do is slow down fear's *momentum* from the start! You want to slow FEAR down before Fear starts getting crazy and ignites a wildfire. And the flames that start off that wildfire the *fastest* are all in the first few minutes of the storm (or the moment you receive the bad news!).

Therefore, once you immediately douse Fear with that first splash of the chemical produced by your laughter—you now have the momentum!

However, you cannot let up! You have to keep your momentum going by keeping this advantage, which simply means you have to apply all the methods, techniques, and knowledge you have learned about Fear in this book:

(1) Fear is False Evidence About Reality—Falsely Envisioning Agonizing Results.

(2) Fear is a LIE and as a LIE it will evaporate in a few seconds.

(3) Fear: If you can PREVENT it—you will END it!

(4) Whatever I Fear Will Appear (**The Magnetic Job- Effect!**).

(5) God works and oftentimes comes through in the 11th hour. Many times as close as 11 hours, 59 minutes and 59 seconds! Therefore, if I have 4-5 days to come up with a response then they've given God and me too much time. Meaning of course, I will make the deadline! At this point, Fear should be packing his bags and searching for a **new victim** because he didn't make a sale at your spiritual or emotional door.

Laughter is a turbocharged chemical, which instantly sends a powerful surge of refreshing, positive chemicals of joy, peace, and happiness. These emotional chemicals will make your whole body feel good very quickly.

Laughter or the chemicals that produce joy, peace and happiness will snap you back-to-life instantly. Laughter is like *smelling salt*—it can wake you up when you lose your consciousness!

Therefore, if you think that Fear is going to win this battle then you have lost your consciousness.

If you believe that Fear is telling the truth and faith is telling this great lie—then you have lost your consciousness.

And if you think, the devil can overrule what God has already promised and approved then you have really lost your consciousness!

Consequently, you really need to laugh—so that by your laughter you will be able to create those special unique chemicals, which will re-energize your mind to take control of this matter and/or situation, quickly.

Laughter produces such a powerful chemical that you can laugh right now and within seconds you will instantly feel a powerful surge of energy overtake you and all of this happens naturally and automatically! You cannot prevent the effects of laughter even if you were to try. Why is this? It is because it is not a trick. It's a fact. It's a universal God-Fact!

Laughter will work whether you foresee its effects coming or not. **A joke may not make you laugh but laughter will always make you laugh!** However, every time you laugh, you are splashing chemicals of joy, peace, and happiness which enter into the spiritual fabric of your soul.

Now, let us put Fear to the same litmus test and see what will happen. Meaning, try to make a *fear-emotion* purely without thought but only by making facial and wide-eye gestures as if you are undergoing or experiencing Fear. What happened? Just as I thought—**NOTHING!** Now, why do you suppose nothing happen? It is because Fear is not *real* whereas laughter is!

Laughter is *real*; Fear is *surreal* (imaginative). For Fear to work you must pull out your mental calculator and begin calculating whether a particular circumstance, situation, and/or event, can cause you some harm, hurt or pain. Fear is almost like a 9 to 5 job, in that you really have to *put in some work*, in order for it to work. For Fear to work it really has to engage in **the mental manipulation-process**—unlike laughter which will work whether you believe it's going to work or not.

Again, You Can Try It Now! Try convincing yourself that the next time you laugh, you are not going to have a chemical surge of positive energy. And I guarantee you that your physiology will not be able to obey this command. The human body will naturally obey the effects of laughter because it is not in its nature to be disobedient to the naturally good things of God.

Yet, for Fear to work—it has to perform mental magic, manipulations or deceptive tricks. For Fear to work it has to be a skilled magician, with a loyal and attentive audience (Mind) in order for it to be influential.

Fear requires three important things in order for it to work:

(1) Fear needs for you to believe it!

(2) Fear needs for you to NOT have an absolute means of preventing it!

(3) Fear needs for you to never give up on fearing it!

On the other hand, laughter doesn't need such cooperation! Laughter doesn't require that you:

(1) Believe it.

(2) Nor does it require that you have a means of preventing it.

(3) Nor does it require that you never give up on it.

Laughter is a beautiful emotional gift that God has given us. It can immediately reward the human spirit with an instant dose of true happiness. Human laughter is an emotional peek into what true happiness really is, in the heavenly state of godliness.

The Power of Laughter

Laughter is famously renowned as one of the world's greatest medicine. There is an old adage which says, "*Music soothes the savage beast.*" Yet I firmly announce that *laughter can soothe the savage beast!*

Laughter is the medicine that one should take 3 or more times a day to alleviate the chronic sickness called Fear.

"*A merry heart doeth good like a medicine.*"
—*Proverbs 17:22.*

The book, *Anatomy of an Illness*, tells the very fascinating real-life story of Norman Cousins—a man who used the awesome power of laughter to overcome a chronic and debilitating illness.

Mr. Cousins' miraculous recovery was based on daily *doses of laughter* as medicine. He watched lots of films, television programs, comedic episodes and he read a bunch of materials that made him laugh. All of this laughter, mostly intense and bellyaching eventually changed him. As a result, he began to feel very optimistic and positive about the course of his illness. This enabled him to sleep better at night, his pain was reduced tremendously and ultimately, his physical condition greatly improved!

The end result of this compelling and real-life story is that Norman Cousins recovered completely, in spite of his doctor's **lack-of-faith** diagnosis, which said that he had a one-in-five-hundred chance of making a full recovery. Fundamentally, The Power of Laughter Prevailed!

For, this seemingly insignificant, mysterious, and very underestimated emotion that many of us **take for granted** was ultimately the key to Mr. Cousins' complete recovery.

The power of laughter basically ignited the healing process! Mr. Cousins had this final statement to say regarding his recovery: *"I have learned never to underestimate the capacity of the human mind and body to regenerate—even when prospects seem most wretched. The life force may be the least understood force on earth."*

This is the *power of laughter*; the least understood and most misunderstood force on earth! Laughter is **free therapy**! It is Mother Nature's way of providing us with a spoonful of *unbottled* medicine to physically, mentally and spiritually heal our most chronic wounds. In the Bible, Jesus recited the Proverb: *"Physician heal thyself (Luke 4:23)."*

So, I guess Norman Cousins got a hold of this proverb and used it to heal himself. Our bodies are a cabinet full of natural medicines and antidotes with no adverse side effects! We have a naturally built-in M.D. and that medical doctor will *out work and out perform* the world's leading physicians by a trillion to one odds any day of the week!

Fear: We Need A Cure

Man still doesn't have a cure for the common cold—let alone, common Fear. The common cold is still being treated with very high dosages of acetaminophen and cough suppressants. How is that, with all this advance medical science and technology, a simple cold is still without a definitive cure?

For the common cold and flu, we're told to take Tylenols, Excedrins, Advils, Thera-flu powders and capsules, etc. **No, Mr. High Technology!** Can we get just *one* product that will do the trick? You guys with your long white coats have been in the laboratories long enough, to at least, come up with a final cure for the common cold.

Where is all the money going in research? We are tired of going to pharmacies buying cough suppressants for our colds. We don't want to **suppress it**—we want to **arrest it!** This is appalling. Yet the same is true with the doctors who attempt to treat their patients with therapy for anxiety attack called "the-cope-with-me" capsule.

For the treatment of anxiety, the majority of therapists echo the same response: *"One must learn how to cope with one's fears."* To **cope** is to **compromise**; to **compromise** is to **tenderize** (soften the effect!). You can't soften the effects of Fear—Fear is the devil!

In all my life, I have never heard of a soft devil! Fear is the devil and it has a very hard, cruel and brutal nature! You can't play with the devil—the devil will kill you! Fear is the devil. You can't **cope** with the devil—you have to **revoke** and **rebuke** him!

Fear is this evil, chemical concoction, which only your mind can create! We have to stop creating this nasty and disgusting chemical called Fear. We are *all physicians* as Jesus clearly stated! We naturally have inside of us, the ability to heal ourselves.

Laughter: One of the Medicines!

Laugher is just one of the medicines of spiritual therapy, which can be used in healing the mental sickness commonly referred to as anxiety (Fear). But you have to shower your spirit with loads of this special chemical, and other spiritual treatments on a daily basis!

Laugher is a type of spiritual shower one ought to take several times each and everyday,. It is a beautiful shower—as it will make your whole body, mind, and spirit incredibly clean (from the dirt of the devil!).

Chapter Twenty-Five

The Emotions of FEAR vs. CONFIDENCE

Fear and Confidence are the only two emotions which start the process of the journey to success or failure. Therefore, which emotion will you choose to accompany you in the journey to success? First, let us define emotions.

Emotions are the physiological or neurological by-products of human thought. It's just that plain and simple! For, all *Motions* come from *E-motions* and all *E-motions* are nothing more than emotional motion. Before you can get into physical motion— you first must be inspired by emotional motion properly called E-motion. E-motion comes by way of thought: the human mind. Human body parts are like dead, inactive dry bones which need life in order to make them work and this is the unique role of e-motions. E-motions give these dead, inactive dry bones their necessary life to perform. There is no *Motion* without *E-motion!*

Fear is *False Evidence About Reality* which *falsely envisions agonizing results!* But, what is confidence? In the word confidence are two words "confide" and "dence". You cannot have confidence without confiding or putting your trust in something. When a man has confidence in winning—he puts his trust in winning. And when a man has confidence in God—he puts his trust in God. Confidence is confiding or putting your trust in. And *dence* really is *dense*, which means **to do it intensely.** Therefore, you must put your trust in God and do it intensely. This is the true meaning of having confidence!

Therefore, God becomes your confidant, or friend you put your confidence in and who will help you navigate on your journey to success. Now, let's begin or prepare for the journey!

So, who all are coming on this journey? How much and what type of luggage will they be bringing? Well, *confidence* is your desired choice but *fear* can't resist coming on this journey. Although, Fear was not originally chosen or invited—he will definitely be present as well.

The pieces of luggage are your emotions! Every individual has an emotional supporting cast. For instance, *Fear's* supporting cast promotes the failure of one's journey and their names are: *disbelief, uncertainty, anxiety, stress, apprehension, sadness, nervousness, worry, and doubt.*

Confidence's supporting cast promotes the success of one's journey and their names are: *belief, faith, certainty, surety, truth, peace, happiness, joy, prosperity, and victory.*

In order to accomplish any goal—you must first map out where you want to go and what will be the necessary tools needed to get you to your desired destination: SUCCESS. And once you have mapped out or decided where you want to go then you are ready to begin your journey on the road to success!

However, on your journey to success, you will inevitably experience days, perhaps even weeks, of bad weather i.e., rain, storms, or even hurricanes.

Moreover, these rough conditions will be so strong and powerful that they will severely affect your sight of the road. Meaning, your vision will experience extreme levels of blurriness to the point that even your defrosters (prayers) will not seem to be working like they should (or like you would have hoped). The roads will be dangerously slippery which means that your tires (support systems) will be sliding every which way. You will not be certain whether you are going to crash or cause a very serious accident! You will feel like you have absolutely NO control of your fate.

Then *emotion-selection* will beckon to come on the scene. So, what emotion might normally be selected when all these things are happening? You guessed it! It is the emotion of Fear and his entire supporting cast.

In such a situation, **Fear** will have you *fearing* a bad accident and perhaps even death; **doubt** will have you *doubting* all situations; and **stress** will keep stressing the issue. Consequently, you will become this nervous wreck! This will make you wonder: *"Why did I bring these bad influences along on this journey anyhow?"*

Truly, all this danger, confusion and turmoil have made you forget that **you didn't invite any of these folks (negative thoughts)**—they just happened to have *welcomed* themselves on a trip that you are paying for emotionally, financially and especially with your life!

However, *confidence* has surfaced and begins to remind you as to why you selected him in the very first place. Its timing could not have been more perfect considering the severe and troubled time you are currently experiencing.

Confidence (or your thoughts confiding intensely with God) says to you: "*Did I not promise you success; And did I not promise you victory? So, why do you fear? For, I AM aware of these weather conditions–AS I WAS THE ONE THAT PRODUCED THEM!* **Fear Not** *as you continue your journey, knowing that I have not forsaken you and that my watchful eye shall forever be protective and mindful of you.*"

The true meaning of *confidence* has re-established and restored your faith in your journey—in spite of the seemingly bleak weather situation up ahead. However, the thing that you must come to realize is that, as you travel from *spiritual state to spiritual state*–**the forecast** will be different—totally different! As sure as night and day, there will be many days of beautifully blazing sunshine!

The Spiritual Journey

"*While the earth remaineth, seedtime and harvest, and cold and heat, and summer and winter, and day and night shall not cease.*"–Genesis 8:22

Seedtime and harvest will never change and will forever remain as constants in the evolution of life. This Universal Law works the same spiritually as it does physically. The seed is the idea (or goal). The harvest is the manifestation of the idea (or goal).

On the spiritual realm, every idea (or goal) that you seek becomes a journey, which will start off like **winter** yet end up like **summer**. Allow me to explain: In winter, it is very cold and it makes you shiver. Likewise, Fear is very cold (callous) and makes you shiver (quiver). Yet confidence or confiding in God will truly keep you warm.

During winter is the time you must develop your idea. Summer marks harvest time (or the time where the idea is developed or completed). Clearly, you are the vehicle that must travel (endure) through the bad weather (trials of life).

Geographically, if you found yourself in a snowstorm in one state—your only relief would be to travel to another state. A "sunshine state" would be a wonderful place to be. On a spiritual level, a person goes from one inward state of being to another until he or she finally reaches that high point in life referred to here as the sunshine state.

Therefore, when you are under a lot of emotional stress—you have to believe that you are going to get to your "sunshine state." When you finally get to that *wonderful place*, you will find the weather (issues of life) will be different—as a matter of fact, beautifully different. So don't worry about today's problems, repossessed car, unpaid bills, failed marriage or relationship. You just need to get to the next *spiritual state* called the "sunshine state" and your entire future will be different. The "sunshine state" is the only spiritual state where you want to be—right about now.

Truly, you have packed and brought too much luggage (hopes and dreams) to think otherwise. Yes, you will enjoy your sunny times (successes). Tomorrow is ordained to be better than yesterday! Therefore, don't be fooled by today's forecast; don't be fooled by the rain, snow or thunderstorm. Your sunny day is tomorrow which will only come after the trials of TODAY!

In *fear*, you will never get there! But with *confidence*, you cannot be **DENIED**. Your aims, goals and purposes in life are already sanctioned and authorized by your heavenly Father within!

Chapter Twenty-Six

FEAR:
The Epilogue

Congratulations! If you have truly understood every chapter in this book then you are officially regarded, as a *Fear Not* advanced student! On the other hand, if you did not quite understand them then you shall remain as a *Fear Not* neophyte (beginner).

As a *Fear Not* neophyte, you must go over those chapters until you gain an understanding so that you can reach the level of an advanced *Fear Not* student.

For one to receive the very powerful *Fear Not* degree official designation—he or she must be a master of all the practical aspects and dimensions of this evil demon called Fear. A *Fear Not* degree master is one who has **a mastered all the false aspects of Fear.**

A master is one who truly understands that all life-situations will include the dynamic fear-factor. The things we experience are nothing more than lessons in life to be learned. A *Fear Not* degree master is one who welcomes and runs towards Fear as opposed to running from it!

A master is one who has truly made the heart and mind connection to the fullest degree. The *Fear Not* degree master understands the very awesome power of the heart. The word HEART has four other words within it! They are:

1. **Ear**
2. **Hear**
3. **He**
4. **Art**

Meaning: It is a spiritual **ART** in which **HE** (man) must use the power of his spiritual **EAR** to spiritually **HEAR** his spiritual **HEART**! For, this is the true meaning of the heart.

Fear Not degree masters are those who truly understand that death and the Fear of death is the last enemy to be destroyed.

"*The last enemy that shall be destroyed is death (1 Corinthians 15:26).*"

Fear Not degree masters are those who can look death right in the face and not flinch a muscle. They already know that the universal science of Fear will magnetically pull them closer to the very thing they're trying to avoid. This is universally known as the *whatsoever you fear—will appear* phenomenon or **The Magnetic Job-Effect.**

In the most extreme cases of Fear or those situations with strong chances of death—the *Fear Not* degree master understands how to uphold the "*Be not weary*" principles to the fullest.

Fear Not degree masters understand that they are not operating *under* the laws of Fear but rather operating *within* the laws of the *Fear Not* dynamic!

Within the laws of the *Fear Not* dynamic, a master already knows that he has a universal *escape clause* from all manners of danger! Meaning what? Meaning, a *Fear Not* degree master can be approaching a seemingly dangerous accident—yet this master of Fear knows how to seize the one millisecond *escape-clause* as if it were an hour!

Spiritually engraved in the heart of every *Fear Not* degree master is this principle: "*The righteous is delivered out of trouble and the wicked cometh in his stead (Proverb 11:8).*"

A *Fear Not* degree master is truly a righteous woman or man of God. The Universal Laws of God will never forsake the *Fear Not* degree master! As it is God who has divinely certified the *Fear Not* degree designation—therefore of course, He (God) has the power to honor His own certificates!

However, in spite of all the things we have written about Fear throughout this book—Fear is really so essential in a very paradoxical way!

Yes, a great portion of this book dealt with how Fear is this terrible monster, this great evil and abomination of man. But contrary to popular belief, Fear is very much needed for the strengthening of who you truly are!

Fear strengthens the character of men and women; and without Fear—you will never know what type of a champion you really are!

Truly, you need a good opponent to bring out the very best in you! Fear is this best opponent for YOU! Fear is naturally the best opposition divinely designed to bring out the greatness in you or the little creator (god) in you.

"Ye are all gods, and all of you are children of the Most High (Psalms 82:6)."

If God is great and *He is*–and if He created us in His image and likeness and *He did* –then we too are great–*this is true.*

But in order for us to be truly great, God had to create for us a great opponent. Thus, Fear became His selection and creation. So, if Fear became God's choice, as this great opponent, then this also means that there is no other opponent, which can be greater!

If you want a weak champion put before him a weak opponent. However, if you should desire a great champion then put before him a great opponent. Fear was created for such a purpose to make you a great champion!

God created Fear to make you great! Yet if Fear happens to defeat you does this loss defeat God's purpose? No, on the contrary–it only defeats yours! God wants you to become a champion–so you really have to beat up this evil force called Fear.

Fear is not as threatening or formidable a foe as you might think. It's just that you have never stood up and fought back! Experts have badly suggested that you cope with him. However, when you finally do decide to stand your ground and fight back—you will notice that you can defeat him!

Well, this is even true in the physical world; school bullies will continue to take your lunch money so long as you let them. But as soon as you stand your ground and fight back—you will see that you can defeat them.

This is the case with Fear. The moment you stand up and are ready to fight is the moment it will be ready to let up and flee. **I repeat, the moment you stand up and are ready to fight is the moment it will be ready to let up and FLEE.**

However, it's a crying shame that we can go through the entire education system (K-12) and then on to college and still not have been taught the truth about Fear. We don't know how to control it or how to master it! **And Yes, Fear Must Be Mastered!**

There's no way on God's green earth should you spend your entire adult life without having dealt with your fears and reached the point of mastering them. That is just horrible! It's like still being in the tenth grade at age 40!

How long should one Fear? Once you have received your championship and/or your character coronation called "the crowning" then that level of Fear is history!

In principle, Fear is to be **leased,** not **financed!** And there is no option to buy—the only option is bye-bye! Fear's future is meant to be fleeting (temporary!). Fear should never be an everlasting part of one's character.

You are the *landlord* and Fear is the *tenant.* Fear should understand that his stay consists of **rent** not **mortgage!** Meaning, once Fear has been used to make you this champion then he must leave! Fear serves no other human purpose!

If Fear should remain beyond its term or expiration date—this can be dangerous! **All levels of Fear have expiration dates!** It is your job to *detect, inspect, and expect* those expiration dates! This means that once a new Fear surfaces—you must *detect it* (acknowledge it); then you must *inspect it* (study it); and finally, you must *expect* (anticipate) its expiration (termination).

Fear is naturally designed to be a great character-builder but historically it has been heralded as this great character-destroyer.

Therefore, identify with your Fears. Don't run from them but instead confront them. Besides, what other way are you to develop as a human being? Please know that the thing that you Fear has a divine assignment! All fears have divine assignments, yet they come dressed in ugly suits!

Every Fear a man or woman has, comes tagged with lessons attached to it—so that they can empower their characters. The life of a *Fear Not* degree master is like that of **an eagle**.

The life of an eagle is an amazing thing to study! When an eagle is faced with a storm—the eagle doesn't run away from the dangers of a storm! On the contrary, the eagle boldly confronts it by spreading its wings and charging into the eye of the storm—in order to use the momentum of the storm to propel itself over and above the storm's dangers.

Fear is the *storm* and you are *the human eagle* that must NOT run from Fear (the storm), but you should lift up your *wings* (embrace it) and begin *charging* (confronting) the *storm* (this fear) and use the *momentum* (the effects) of the storm to propel *you* (lift you) over and above it (to victory!).

This is exactly how Fear should be handled and applied in one's life. This is the lesson that everyone must **MASTER!**

Mastering Fear really is not that difficult once you get used to it. At first, Fear can seem very intimidating and difficult to manage. But once you understand that it is just a process and a lesson for you to learn—you will be on your way to ultimately overcoming it. You must be convinced that your **winning empowerment** within will eventually begin lessening the effects of this fear—thereby, enabling you to defeat it completely!

Again, Fear is a great character-builder and its stay is only temporary! *Tarry* means to delay or stay temporarily. Fear should only stay temporarily. This is why you must be *an electri-tarian* which means LET U **tarry** HIM. You must *tarry* or let Fear stay just until he completes the assignment of making you a spiritual champion of God.

Once that is done then you must immediately **evict him** and call it:

RENT OVERDUE!!!

May God Bless You!

FINAL WORD!

When you have finally mastered Fear, the days of the devil ruling you will be completely over! A *Ph.D.* of any kind is not bestowed with this divine God-power within. So, now it's official:

A
Fear Not!
Degree
Is better than
A
Ph.D.

However, a Ph.D. recipient accompanied with a *Fear Not* degree is a very brilliant combination! Without a Fear Not degree, a Ph.D. beholder loses a great inner power and is vulnerable to great defeats.

However, if you have them both (Fear Not Degree and a Ph.D.) then you are truly a fine representation of the awesome power of God. But always remember that your *Fear Not* degree is a greater authority than your Ph.D.!

God Bless!

Fifteen (15) Lessons On FEAR:

1. Flying On Airplanes.

2. A Critical Hospital Report Or News.

3. Eviction.

4. Business Venture.

5. Speaking Or Singing Before Large Crowds.

6. A Big Game.

7. Shyness: A Form of Fear.

8. Agoraphobia and OCD.

9. Problematic Phobia.

10. Phobia Of Strange Noises, etc.,

11. Fear and Logic.

12. The Fear of Death.

13. Fear is The Greatest Sin!

14. Prayer versus Fear.

15. Fear Returned!

Lesson One

Flying On Airplanes
(Part One)

Question #1: I know that commercial plane accidents have nearly a less than one percent chance of occurring. Yet I always Fear that this less than one percent chance will one day include me! How can I over come this Fear?

Answer: First of all, don't allow yourself to think that you will succumb to this bad statistic! Consider yourself a blessed member of God's family. Therefore, don't think this poorly of yourself. For, death doesn't call anyone—it is people that call and cause death. So, don't *call or cause* your death but *call and cause* your life as God is your Protector.

Death has its separate road and life has its separate road as well. Life and death are not freeways which merge, crossover or overlap. Death cannot make a decision about life; life cannot make a decision about death, but man and woman decides them both!

In the pathway of life there are no exits and in the pathway of death there are no exits. It is people that make these exits! The Bible says: "*In the way of righteousness is life; and in the pathway thereof there is no death (Proverbs 12:28).*"

Question #2: I am terrified when the plane undergoes turbulence. How must I overcome this Fear?

Answer: Well, let's go deeper than the whole turbulence thing, because your phobia is much deeper than that! If you are on a plane that happens to be experiencing turbulence—you have only one major concern: "*Are you really on a safe plane?*" Moreover, you would like to know: "*Can you really trust the mechanical laws regarding this aircraft and can you trust the spiritual laws of formlessness called air in which it is governed?*"

Many people spend over 99% of their lifetime on the ground (the physical realm) and less than 1% flying on planes (the formless or spiritual realm). Flying on planes is truly feeling faith physically! So if you ever wanted a physical description of what faith feels like then take a trip on an airplane!

Many people regard the very act of flying as a horrifying experience. Why is this, you may ask? It is because, in spite of our education, many of us were never taught how to properly deal with this type of Fear. And the people who fear the act of flying the most are the most intelligent people on the planet! However, these very same people have never had a lesson on Fear in the face of absolute formlessness.

In our education system, there was no "*How To Control One's Fear of Flying*" curriculum for them to depend on as a navigational guide. It was never taught on the elementary, high school and/or collegiate level.

In the act of flying, the management of one's Fear is a new and different curriculum which requires a new and different crop of teachers to teach it!

Yes, many people Fear the BIG voyage in the air! This voyage in the air is purely spiritual. Air is a spirit and a spirit is *formless*. The spiritual realm that governs air is properly called absolute *formlessness*. So, the real question is "*Do you fear physical form or absolute formlessness?*" Do you feel safer when your body is operating on *physical form* (land) than operating on the spiritual realm of *absolute formlessness* (air)? There are many men and women of faith who feel safer in the air—than they do on land.

However, when *unfaithful* men and women board an airplane, it becomes a very frightening experience. Why? It is because they have just left or departed from their god called physical *form*. So, just like the child whose mother has left him in the room alone—they are terrified and silently crying in great apprehension as they experience the operation of a plane in progress.

The *unfaithful* people of the laws of formlessness fear the very act of flying simply because they have just parted ways with their deity or **god-guardian on the ground** called physical land. Truly, man fears that which is outside the physical realm of its god. Well, that's a spiritual mistake on their parts!

Unfortunately, this is the price one must pay when you rely on or put your hopes in a very limited physical god. The scriptures say, "*For he that soweth to his flesh shall of the flesh reap corruption; but he that soweth of the spiritual shall of the spirit reap life everlasting (Galatians 6:8).*"

The modern translation: He that soweth (believes) to his flesh (the physical realm) shall of the flesh reap corruption (anxiety and fear), but he (or she) that soweth (believe) of the spiritual (the formless realm) shall reap life everlasting (long lasting life with all the sweet juices of Divine Protection!). This is **The Modern Translation!**

Therefore, turbulence is nothing but *speed bumps* in the air! You have never had any fear about going over speed bumps on land—so why get emotionally bent out of shape over speed bumps in the air. **A bump is a bump** no matter what level it is on, whether on the ground or in the air! So, just relax, stay cool because everything is going to be fine. Turbulence and the whole act of flying is nothing to a *Fear Not* degree student or master. It is just a reminder of the expression of faith and the power of controlling one's Fear in the face of anything! This is all just a part of your lesson. So, please, **PASS THE TEST!**

Question #3: My new job requires a lot of out-of-state travel, primarily flying yet I have a great Fear of flying. What should I do?

Answer: The first thing you need to do is to welcome this new challenge and opportunity with opens arms! Second, this new job will be a great and daily exercise of all the things that you are learning in the mastery of human Fear.

Therefore, let's get right to the point! You said that you are absolutely terrified about the idea of flying. And unquestionably, you would probably prefer choosing to use a car, bus or even a train rather than flying. Am I correct? Okay, let's deal with the facts: Your chances of dying from a plane crash are less than one percent. Your chances of dying from a car accident are about 30 to 40 percent! So, would it make you feel any safer to learn that flying on an airplane is purely 99.99% safe? Well, this nearly perfect statistic would be very satisfactory to me. **However, it is a gross understatement!** The true statistics say that flying on a commercial plane is actually 99.9999996% safe!!! This aviation report further asserts that you will stand a much greater chance of dying from a fall off a ladder than you would from a plane crash. This is true!

Question #4: *How can I be sure that God will pay attention to little ole me as I prepare to board a plane?*

Answer: Jesus said: "*But even the very hairs of your head are all numbered. FEAR NOT therefore (Luke*

12:7)." What Jesus is simply saying is that God pays close attention to every *single* detail. Therefore, in spite of being in the midst of six billion people— **God Sees You!** He knew you had boarded this plane—as He was the ONE who authorized the ticket! So, it doesn't matter where you sit, because just like each, single strand of hair that God *personally* numbered—He also has numbered YOU!

In other words, you are under God's spiritual surveillance and are divinely protected from all manner of hurt or harm and even death! **Thus, Enjoy Your Flight!**

Flying On Airplanes Pt. 2
(The Science of Stillness)

Fear has only one goal: **Attack The Human Nervous System!** However, it is impossible for Fear to be truly effective when you have a steady, cool, calm, and peaceful nervous system.

"The less nervous your BRAIN the more control you'll GAIN!"

In the Bible, it reads: *"But let him ask in faith, nothing wavering. For, he that wavereth is like a wave of the sea driven with the wind and tossed (James 1:6). "*

Turbulence is a wave of the air and we should not be driven by its wind nor should we allow it to toss us (or make us emotionally shiver). The above scripture says: *"But let him ask in faith, nothing wavering"* which simply means don't *tremble*, don't *shiver*, and don't *shake!*

If you are nervous about flying on planes then you must control your nervous system. It's the nervous system that causes a person to *tremble, shiver, or shake*—as there is not another place within man where this can otherwise be done. Therefore, it is very important to capture what is called **The Still Spirit!**

In principle, Fear is killed when the spirit is still! If you want to receive the *real spirit*—you have got to achieve the *still spirit*. Being *still* will bring this spirit for *real*. The Bible recommends *stillness* against our enemies who are actually our *inner-me's*:

*"Ye approach this day unto battle against your enemies: let not your heart faint, **Fear Not,** and do not tremble (Deuteronomy 20:3)."*

"Be still, and know that I am God (Psalms 46:10)."

Yes, *stillness* is the key, which unlocks the prison system called Fear. Again, Fear is *killed* when the spirit is *still!*

Therefore, when you are on the plane practice the *art of stillness*. Put your mind, your thoughts, and your emotions into a state of stillness and this will stimulate your body and soul to a supernatural state of supreme stillness.

The heart is the common denominator and it ultimately determines the extent of this stillness.

The heart is a true tattletale, in that, it will truthfully **tattle** anything that is **telling** (revealing!).

"Let us draw near with a true heart in full assurance of faith (Hebrews 10:22)."

True assurance of faith is recorded in the heart! The heart will amplify and re-play the rhythm of your faith and will accurately magnify what you truly believe or believe not.

The heart is the best **witness** to your **stillness.** The heart is this remarkable non-lying, spiritual system that will reveal whether or not your spirit is *still.* So, you may be pretty clever and crafty at fooling other people but you will never—AND I MEAN NEVER be able to outsmart or fool this beautiful thing called *your heart.* For this spiritual thing called the heart always tells the truth all the time. *The heart* is the world's greatest witness! And these are very important words to remember as you prepare for your flight.

Thus, if you want to really keep it REAL then really keep it STILL!

Flying On Airplanes Pt. 3
(The "Peace, Be Still" Science)

I would love to go right into this lesson. But I would not be doing my duty, if I were NOT to give you one of history's greatest lessons on Fear versus forces of nature.

It was two thousand years ago when Jesus taught a great mystery, the science of faith's superiority over fear in *an aviation-like* test to his twelve disciples. However, this was not **a written test**. Oh no! This was **a road test!** The Bible describes the details in the book of Mark chapter 4:35-41:

(35) *"And the same day, when the even was come, he saith unto them, Let us pass over unto the other side.*

(36) *And when they had sent away the multitude, they took him even as he was in the ship. And there were also with him other little ships.*

(37) *And there arose a great storm of wind, and the waves beat into the ship, so that it was now full.*

(38) And he was in the hinder (rear) part of the ship, asleep on a pillow: and they awake him, and say unto him, Master, carest thou not that we perish (or die)?

(39) And he rose, and rebuked the wind, and said unto the sea, **Peace, be still.** And the wind ceased, and there was a great calm.

(40) And he said unto them, Why are ye so fearful? How is it that ye have no faith?

(41) And they feared exceedingly, and said one to another, What manner of man is this, that even the wind and the sea obey him?"

In the midst of the deep seas, Jesus put his disciples to a test. Truly, this was an *on-the-job* training type of test where (Jesus) the instructor was out to see whether his disciple's **power of faith** would be able to subdue their power of fear.

It is very important that we point out that traveling at sea can be just as dangerous as traveling in air! Whether you are taking a voyage in the deep of the oceans or high in the earth's atmosphere called air—there is one thing they both have in common: "*You are in the middle of no where and there is no land in sight!* "

Another important factor they both have in common is: *"Neither can afford the slightest failure!"* The ship cannot afford the slightest failure in the water (the force of nature on which it heavily depends) just as the plane cannot afford the slightest failure in the air (the force of nature on which it heavily depends).

Both of these passenger-vehicles have to have perfect trips to and fro. The ship in the *sea* and the plane in the *air* have the same threat potential and only differ in the forces of nature they travel through.

Therefore, the trip that Jesus decided for his disciples on the ship was our version of an airplane. It had the same **threat potential** as an airplane; it had the same *"middle-of-no-where* and *there-is-no-land-in-sight"* **feature** as an airplane. Also, it had the same *"I can 't-afford-to-fail"* **demand** as an airplane. So, two thousand years ago, Jesus disciples experienced **Our Modern Day Flight!**

However, there were some very compelling details regarding the nature of the disciple's journey versus the average person's experience on an airplane.

For instance, the disciples were dangerously confronted with a ship filled with water! Therefore, for Jesus to have not been affected by this water, only suggests to us that Jesus had to have been not only in the hinder (or rear area), as the biblical text clearly states—but on a higher, or raised platform. Yet the point remains, the ship on which the disciples were traveling was filled with water!

Now, the average person flying on a plane will not be going through this type of experience at all. Remember, the disciples had water in the ship! Plus, the water was overflowing.

For the average person on a plane, the greatest air-threat is **the self-adjusted, air ventilated button situated in the upper compartment (and the person has the pleasure to turn on or off at its convenience)!** This is the average passenger's greatest air-threat! Wow, scary business, you may say? Yeah, right! I can hardly imagine how threatening that can turn out to be.

Candidly, I must say to you my friend: "*If you are currently on an airplane and the windows are still in tact and not broken out—then you need to chill out and relax because the lesson you are going through is chicken scrap and no where near or close to the lesson and terror that the disciples had to go through."* **Remember, they had water in the ship!** Plus, the water was overflowing. Yet what do you have? Well quite frankly, you just have the self-adjusted, conveniently placed, air vent in the upper compartment, which is at your convenience!

The second compelling detail of this same lesson is in verses 39 to 41:

*(39) "And he rose, and rebuked the wind, and said unto the sea, **Peace, Be Still.** And the wind ceased, and there was a great calm.*

(40) And he said unto them, Why are ye so fearful? How is it that ye have no faith?

(41) And they feared exceedingly, and said one to another, What manner of man is this, that even the wind and the sea obey him?"

The thing that concerned Jesus in this lesson was: *"Why did the disciples awaken him for their road test?* This was not a road test to examine Jesus' abilities, as his powers had already been divinely proven! Clearly, this journey was exclusively a test for them! It was the responsibility of the twelve disciples to bring those roaring winds and violent waves to a calm.

For years, Jesus had been vigorously teaching his twelve disciples the spiritual tools, concerning *faith and the tongue,* and the power they can bring if joined together!

In the Bible, Jesus taught this **"Faith and Tongue"** lesson to his disciples: *"If ye had FAITH as a grain of mustard seed, ye might SAY unto this sycamine tree, be thou plucked up by the root, and be thou planted in the sea; and it should obey you (Luke 17:6)."* The other faith and tongue lesson in which Jesus taught his disciples was: *"Death and life are in the power of the tongue (Proverb 18:21)."*

Just recently, I read where biologists have asserted that the strongest muscle in the human anatomy is the tongue!

Faith and The Tongue Get Things Done!

You may be a person who has yet to make this strong *faith* and *tongue* connection; and one who still believes that it going to take time before you are able to apply the very powerful, **"Peace, be** still" commandment to calmly end your earthly storms.

However, bestowed within you is this awesome ability to apply the very powerful "**Peace, be still**" commandment to calmly end the emotional storm in your mind called the Fear of flying! And so, this brings us to the preparation of the flight. So, are you ready?

Very good! From this point forward, I will be giving you step-by-step details on what to do and what not to do while the flight is getting prepared for takeoff. So for now, I want for you to put this book down and resume reading it just as soon as the plane is on the runway and about to take flight. So, bye for now!

—Intermission—

Flying On Airplanes Pt. 3 cont
(Back from Intermission)

Okay, you're back! So, I take it that the plane is ready for take off and it is at this point that the **"Peace, be still"** exercise and lesson is officially in effect! Therefore, I want you to pay close attention to this lesson. So, are you ready? Well, let us begin:

STEP I

As soon as the plane is off the ground and making its voyage into one of the universe's safest zones of formlessness, which we humans call air—I would like for you to relax, be calm, stay cool, and enjoy the flight—as I *fear coach* you until you are at least fairly comfortable with your flight.

So, how are you feeling so far? Are you a little nervous? Well, you have no reason to be, because a supremely Higher Force is now watching over you, and this *double-engine* plane, to assure that it reaches its final destination safely and soundly.

Now, what I would like for you to do, at this point, is to look at everyone on the plane and say silently or in a low tone: *"All of you are blessed that*

I'm on this plane. My very presence will assure a safe, secure, and protected flight, by the very Supreme Power on which this plane is solely depended. Again, all of you here are truly blessed that I have boarded this plane!"

During, the first few minutes of the plane's takeoff, the plane will encounter *slight turbulence* as it seeks the appropriate clear path to its desired destination. As the pilot searches for this clear path—the plane is going to feel like it's having some type of engine complication or it may seem like it's about to shut down but this is truly not the case. The plane is just experiencing some turbulence right now. So, be calm and everything will be fine. In a little while, a smooth path will be emerging.

When the plane has finally established its clear path and is *turbulence-free*, the captain and/or flight attendant will signal that its okay to unfasten the seat belt and this is normally the time, for the passengers on board, to pull out their laptops, use the lavatories, etc. Then, food, drinks, and other refreshments may be served. This leads us to our next phase of this same lesson which is . . .

STEP II

Now, in the second phase of this lesson, we are going to **simulate** the two thousand year old lesson that Jesus gave his disciples—as we *modernize it* and give it a twenty-first century twist! So right now, I would like for you to press the service button in the upper compartment above your head and ask one of the very nice flight attendants (well, I hope they're nice) for a cup of water.

The thing that I would like for you to do is to hold this cup of water in your hand and bring *stillness* to the water inside. However, do not put away this book! You must be able to still read as you perform this exercise. Periodically, I would like for you to glance over at the cup to monitor the balance and steadiness of the water inside.

If there is no *stillness* to this cup of water then you must put this book down and begin totally focusing on what is physiologically going on inside of you and what is preventing this cup of water from reaching a satisfactory state of stillness. I use the word "satisfactory" purposely because I'm keeping in mind, the natural momentum and/or vibrations of the plane itself.

However, you should still be able to balance or bring some stillness to the cup of water in spite of this obvious fact.

The exercise I would like for you to do now is to mentally address that special part of your brain called *the nervous system*. Say in a very commanding and authoritative tone of voice: **"Peace, be still."**

I would like for you to keep repeating to yourself this very powerful commandment: **"Peace, be still"** until you have finally brought some stillness to this *uncalmed* cup of water.

Remember, you are currently engaged in a modernized two thousand year old *"Peace, be still"* lesson and Jesus is still the instructor because *he lives in us!* So, do a far better job with this lesson than the disciples and bring these raging waters to a state of calmness and without having to call out for *Jesus* to do a job that we have the very power to do ourselves.

Therefore, apply the **"Peace, be still"** spiritual method on these raging waters, (referred to here as your nerves and emotions), which you are experiencing within! This brings us to...

Step III

This part of the lesson deals with **the heart barometer principle** and its relationship with *the nervous system*. How are you feeling so far, after having gone through both step one and two? Well, I'm confident that you are doing more than fine as I continue to walk you through these very simple principles of mastering one's Fears.

With no further delay, let us go right on to the next part of this lesson, which deals with *the heart*. Now, you have to pay close attention to the heart and its **throbbing beats!** Those beats will reveal the entire *physiological* story! If your heart is rapidly throbbing, the beats are sending messages to your brain that say: *"You are mentally uncertain and have no faith in your present situation."* And the harder your heart throbs to this apparent uncertainty the greater the Fear!

In this phase of the lesson, the heart's overall purpose is to measure the *emotional temperature* of the climate of your mind!

If you are not doing a good job of maintaining a steady calm, **mental climate** then the heart is going to reveal it!

The harder and faster your heart beats the more your nervousness system is out of control. And consequently, you will begin noticing the cup of water trembling like crazy. It is your job to establish peace and calm within your nervous system (which is the main area within the temple of God) and establish it immediately!

Your ultimate goal is to keep the cup of water as *still* as possible throughout the turbulence. Practically, this can be done by stiffening the area and energy around your heart and commanding it to be *still*. What you are actually doing is sending a direct message to the brain, which then delivers this message to the mind. The mind accepts the message and begins producing brain chemicals to honor this command. All of this should restore peace, calm, and stability to your nervous system, thereby, giving you self-control over this particular phase of Fear (fear of turbulence).

An excellent model to emulate for the best example of a **"Peace, be still"** ability is our planet earth. The earth rotates at a speed of over one thousand and thirty seven miles per hour! However, the amazing thing is that you cannot feel the vibrations of such remarkable speed at all.

The earth appears to be steady, still and unmoving, but the opposite is true. Yet, there are a lot of demands of tremendous vibrations that constantly challenge the earth's steadiness or stillness. However, the earth knows how to naturally do what we humans must learn to do mentally and spiritually.

The earth has a built-in **"Peace be still"** cruise control system! We, humans, have a similar system. Yet the cruise control system that we have is spiritual. Fortunately, this spiritual system doesn't need to be developed or created—the only thing we have to do is *activate it!* The only thing we have to do is click the right spiritual switch and this incredibly beautiful, cruise control-system will spiritually activate its **"Peace be still"** features automatically!

No matter how much turbulence you are experiencing or how badly the pilot is flying the plane—there is no degree of turbulence so great that it will disturb the uniquely designed **"Peace be still"** cruise control system called *the human nervous system.*

The human nervous system is your control center. Therefore, anytime you are going through intense moments of fear during turbulence, the only thing you have to do is spiritually **click the switch!** When you do that you can go through five straight hours of brutal turbulence and sweetly sleep through it all, while the rest of passengers are trembling in fear, sitting on pins and needles, or having a conniption fit!

So, whenever turbulence is occurring just **CLICK THE SWITCH!**

Flying On Airplanes pt. 4

You have just completed the **"Peace be still"** physical version of the exercise, which required that you read these chapters while simultaneously observing yourself bringing balance to the cup of water.

Now, you will be asked to put the book away and begin the **"Peace be still"** mental and/or imaginary version of this exercise. This will require that you mentally playback everything you've read in these chapters in clear and specific details. After you have completed the **"Peace, be still"** mental version—I would like for you to prepare to take a very nice nap and be like Jesus. Meaning, when the rest of the disciples were in terror about the dangers of the plight—Jesus was asleep on a pillow! Thus, like your big brother Jesus—I would like for you to grab a pillow, lay back AND GET SOME SLEEP!

"When thou liest down, thou shalt not be afraid: yea, thou shalt lie down, and thy sleep shall be sweet (Proverbs 3:24)."

ENJOY YOUR FLIGHT!

Lesson Two

A Critical Hospital Report Or News

Question: *I have just learned that a friend has been seriously hurt and is in the hospital. What should be the first thing I do?*

Answer: PRAY! PRAY! PRAY! Praying to God should be the very first thing you should be doing.

The very next thing you need to do is to put your emotional state at peace before you even attempt to walk out the door. The third thing you need to do is to not think about the worst-case scenario! Meaning, don't begin to consider outcomes that consist of a permanent handicap, paralysis or other serious injuries. And definitely, don't consider the possibility of death!

Keep your thoughts very positive and negative-free. This is not the time you want the *Magnetic Job-Effect* to come into play! Another factor that you must be prepared to deal with is: Do not allow any one around you to talk about death or some other terrible outcome. And if a family member, or friend is hollering and screaming uncontrollably—please calm them down immediately as this may trigger your emotional state in the wrong direction.

After you have properly established a solid spiritual, mental, and emotional state—then, you are ready to make your way to the hospital. As you make your way there believe that God has already answered your prayers and is the **New Physician** on the scene!

As you travel to the hospital here are your step-by-step instructions: Take five deep breaths and get yourself very relaxed and pay very close attention to all the little details as you head for the hospital.

First thing that I would like for you to do is **place the key** into the ignition very *calmly*; **turn the key** in the ignition *calmly*; and **pull out of** the driveway or parking space *calmly*. *Do not rush* to the hospital instead *drive* carefully, slowly and calmly. Besides, you are not a doctor and even if you are a doctor, you don't have this patient's assignment.

So, relax, stay calm and monitor all your emotions of anxiety (Fear).The more you remain in this serene state, the more you will have the positive forces and energies to assist in bringing about a positive result!

Lesson Three

Eviction

Question: *I just received a court eviction notice that mandated that my three children and I vacate within three days! I'm terrified about the thought of my children and I being kicked out on the streets. How can I keep my Fear under control while I come up with the necessary money to prevent this eviction notice?*

Answer: The first thing you need to do is to go to your source of power, which is within! Meditate within this Universal Power or Force and ask it to assist you with your situation. This is properly defined as prayer. Upon completion of your Universal Request, you must now do all you can to come up the finances to prevent this impending eviction. For, prayer without work is dead (James 2:17).

With your prayers, it is very important to NOT place the eviction notice first—but on the contrary—make it your **last request to God!**

Remember, Fear demands priority. Fear loves being put first so purposely put the request about the eviction LAST on your prayer agenda.

This approach sets the stage of bringing these emotions of fear under complete control.

Moreover, you are sending yourself a message that you are relaxed and in full control about this whole eviction-situation. And your proof of being in spiritual control of the matter is that you placed this eviction request last. This is key!

The Second Key is to make it seem as though you almost forgot to mention it. Fear hates this! When one does this Fear says: *"How dare you? How dare you place me last when I should be the first thing on your list? How dare you?*

Just to rub it in more emphatically end your prayer with: *"Oh, by the way, I almost forgot, I have this eviction coming up within three days and Father please help me gather the necessary finances to prevent this from happening. Thank you Heavenly Father."*

Oh, Fear is burning, twisting and twirling in anger! Fear cannot believe that you placed it last. Well, by putting Fear last means Fear is that much closer to its next step, which is clearly out the door, and that translates to mean it is clearly **Out of Your Mind—Plus Spirit!**

Lesson Four

FEAR of a Business Venture

A leopard cannot change its spots! Fear is a spiritual leopard, which cannot change its spiritual spots. Fear's suggestions are filled with deceptive, doubtful or *spotted lies* and such lies will never change! Fear is *False Evidence About Reality–Falsely Envisioning Agonizing Results* from the beginning all the way to the end! Fear is a lie.

Here is how it works from a *business venture* perspective: Let's say that you want to start your own business. However, you would need to take out a loan for five thousand dollars ($5,000). Immediately, Fear comes into the picture and says to you: "*You might as well forget about trying to apply for $5,000 because you're not going to get approved for this loan due to your terrible credit!*" Yet, in spite Fear's negative suggestion, you applied for the loan anyhow. By the grace of God, you were approved the following week and the monies are already in your account. **Thus, you've now challenged and defeated LIE number one.**

At this point, you now have the plan, purpose, and necessary finances to jump-start your own business and are prepared to put things into action. However, Fear steps into the picture again. It now says to you: *"I see that you got the loan. However, I already told you that the business you're starting cannot succeed in this vicious business environment. Even your family, relatives and closest friends have warned you that this business venture was a bad idea. So, my humble advice to you is that you stop everything, while you still have some money left. And besides, at least you wouldn't have the entire $5,000 to pay back when the company flops."*

Remember, a leopard cannot change its spots! Fear is *False Evidence About Reality–Falsely Envisioning Agonizing Results* from the beginning all the way to the end! In spite of yet another one of Fear's negative suggestions—the business is a success and is reaping great dividends. **So, you've now challenged and defeated LIE number one.**

However, Fear steps into the picture once more and now says: *"Yeah, your little business is doing really good but because you are so busy with your business situations—you are seldom home and spending less time with your wife. And since you haven't been around as often—I wouldn't put it past her to have found someone else to intimately occupy her where you have failed! So, you really need to be concerned about this and take immediate action NOW!"*

However, these adulterous implications were later proven to be just another boldfaced LIE. Fear was just desperately trying to get a victory in the win column. Fear actually hated how you stood your ground and maintained your determination to be successful! Therefore, Fear made these feeble attempts trying to disturb the mind and spirit of a very determined man, who was reaping remarkable success in spite of Fear's relentless and negative attacks.

So, the point one must learn from this lesson is that Fear (devil) never stops in his negative attempts to distract. Had you believed him on his *first attempt—*you would have never applied for the loan. Had you believed him at that *second attempt—*you would never have continued the pursuit of the business venture. Finally, had you believed in his very desperate last attempt to try to cause strife between you and your wife—you would have given yourself up to self-torture, self-incrimination and wrongfully misjudging a beautiful wife and a very happy marriage.

The devil is a LIE and Fear is his NAME!

Lesson Five

Speaking or Singing Before Large Crowds

Question: *I'm very nervous about performing or giving speeches before large crowds. What must I do to get rid of this Fear?*

Answer: The first thing that must be established is how you see the outcome! The only thing that you fear is that you will not perform well or to your best abilities. Am I correct? This is the extent of your fear!

For the most part, if you do not already have singing or oratorical talent then overcoming Fear is not going to improve where such talent never existed. However, if you do have the talent or skill as a singer or communicator, then fearing *can* and *will make* you appear untalented! Overall, this is not the outcome you want. **Embarrassment Is The Great Fear Here!**

Your fear is this: *You don't want to shame or make a complete fool of yourself!* But one of the good things about having true talent is that, it can rescue you in troubled times and save you from an impending disaster of humiliation! Remember, Fear is a LIE and will evaporate like smoke!

If you're the type of person who can comfortably sing or communicate with just *one person* in the auditorium, then if *a second person* comes in will this intimidate you? What about *a third person* coming in? Well, that's all a thousand people in a room represents—it is *this same one person multiplied by one thousand!* The nine hundred and ninety ninth (999th) person is not **nine hundred and ninety nine people**—he or she is just one person in a room with a whole lot of other *ones* and that is what makes up this group of one thousand. Okay, so, RELAX!

Remember, your audience is not the least bit intimidated by watching you perform. So why should you be intimidated with performing in front of them?

They didn't come to see you *fear*—they came to see YOU perform your good talents. Fear wasn't on the menu—so don't serve it! Fear is a whole different show. So, please, don't give the audience something that they didn't come to see.

Truly, Fear is not who they came to see! They came to see YOU and not Fear. **So, Please, Do Not Do A Duet With The Devil.** Meaning what?

For instance, let's say you name is Kelly and the host of the show was to make this announcement: *"Ladies and gentlemen, please, give a nice and warm welcome to our next performer Kelly featuring Fear!"* Truly, this is a performer's worst nightmare!

Featuring FEAR will mess up your CAREER!

Don't let Fear rob your show. This is your gig! Tell Fear to get his own and his own audience while he's at it! Remember, this audience belongs to YOU! Now go handle your business and give your audience an outstanding, wonderful and fantastic show because they deserve it AND SO DO YOU!!!

I Am Counting On You—So, FEAR NOT!

Lesson Six

The Big Game

Question: *I have a very big game tomorrow and I'm so nervous that I can't even sleep. What can I do about this fear?*

Answer: First, you need to go to bed and get as must rest as possible—that way, you will have a fresh flow of energy and relaxed nerves with which to participate.

Remember, the other team is just as nervous about the big game as you. However, the team that has the better control of their nerves WILL WIN the game!

I have played against people who had a competitive edge over me but because they were so nervous about the game—they wound up losing and losing terribly. Why? It was because nervousness takes away a person's competitive edge.

I have discovered that if a person has a 30% talent advantage over you—this puts you at a negative thirty (-30). But if he or she is very nervous about the game that nervousness will increase your talent level to plus fifty (+50). So, in effect, you have actually gained an advantage of 20% (-30 – +50 = +20). And if you can keep this *anxiety-free* momentum going—you will ultimately secure the victory!

When people cannot control their nervousness, it can literally cost them their competitive edge and victory. This brings us to this point:

Personal Stats Mean Nothing When You Are Personally Tormented By Fear.

Even if the other team is stacked to the ceiling in the talent-department—you must remain confident. Do not faint, flinch, nor worry. Why? Because this is a big game and big games magnetize great Fear. Great Fear paralyzes great men and great teams! So, it is okay that a team has more talent than yours—just so long as this talent-advantage doesn't display itself during **the actual game!**

It is truly an honor to make it to the big game and if your team made it to this point—then obviously your team is not some group of slouches.

Slouches cannot make it to a big game—they are eliminated way before they get to this point! So, if your team made it to the big game, then obviously your team is to be reckoned with and not to be taken lightly.

Remember, the theme of our subject matter is not *big games*—**It's The Big Game!** All your team needs to do is to win just ONE GAME and then you guys can celebrate your victory big time.

Therefore, allow a team to gloat over their competitive edge commonly referred to as **stats**. But have every member of your team live by this *esprit de corps* (team spirit) motto:

"A team can be regarded as the best team BEFORE the game and even regarded as the best team AFTER the game but just don't let them be regarded as the best team DURING the game!!!"

Godspeed!

Lesson Seven

Shyness: A Form of Fear

Question: Can you define the word **SHY** for me?

Answer: According to Webster's New World Dictionary, the word *shy* is defined as follow:

1. easily frightened or startled; timid. 2. not at ease with other people; extremely self-conscious; bashful. 3. showing distrust or caution; **wary.**

However, if you were to take all three definitions and convert them into one—you will come to the characteristic nature of the devil. *Shy* simply means Satan Harassing You!

Question: *Is that it?*

Answer: Not at all! The full and complete definition of the word *shy* is as follow:

Satan
Harassing
You

Subtly
Humiliating
You

(by)

Silently
Hindering
Your expressiveness!

This Is The True Meaning Of Being SHY!!!

Lesson Eight

Agoraphobia and OCD

An agoraphobic is clinically defined as a person who fears being in open (public) places. In the word "agoraphobia" is the word *agora*, which comes from the Greek word *"ageirein"* and it means *to assemble*. *Phobia* is a Greek term as well and it comes from the word *"phobos"* which means fear. When you combine the two terms, they mean *"to assemble fear."* Therefore, agoraphobia has no special significance to open places—it only has significance to assembling fear.

In today's world, agoraphobics do nothing but assemble or gather tons and tons of fear. Defining agoraphobia, as a fear of open or public places is definitely a wrong diagnosis. This will consequently precipitate a wrong prognosis!

OCD

An OCD patient is clinically defined as a person with an Obsessive Compulsive Disorder.

However, the true definition of an OCD patient is a person who performs abnormal rites, rituals and routines, which are excessive in nature—due to **personal inoculation of self-superstition** which is based on his or her fears (whether consciously or sub-consciously).

The shorter version is simply a person who afflicts oneself with self-created superstition. This person believes that if he or she DOES NOT perform certain and/or specific rituals that it will somehow *spell* a bad omen or amount to some misfortune. Consequently, this type of mind compels this person to fear.

If there is an error in the diagnosis then there will be many severe errors in the prognosis. So, what is clinically characterized as OCD is purely self-superstition and everything else is just one's reaction to it.

Therefore, to characterize an OCD patient as a person who has *an obsessive compulsive disorder* is only asserting one's reaction to it! **Again, characterizing an OCD patient as a person who has an obsessive compulsive disorder is only asserting one's reaction to it!** OCD is not a definition of a disorder but merely a description of it! Clinically, the term OCD must be redefined if it aims to cure.

Fear is an OCD, CD and a D.

Fear is an OCD because it is *obsessive*; it is *compulsive*; and it is definitely a *disorder*.

Fear is a CD, which means it's *a chronic disease*. Fear is a disease, which endures for a great number of years and oftentimes even a lifetime.

Fear is a D or *a disorder*, which converts into an absolute deadly disease.

Therefore, **FEAR** is the only thing, which can be diagnosed as an OCD but never the PATIENT!

Wrong Diagnosis—Wrong Prognosis!

Lesson Nine

Problematic Phobia

Question #1: *I have an existing problem that is causing me great Fear. How should I go about handling this problem?*

Answer: First, Fear may not have been the reason for your problem because your problem may solely have been a product of **a bad decision**. However, Fear is definitely the reason if the matter is continuously getting worse. Fear is not always the reason why problems begin but Fear is most often the reason why they never end.

Therefore, if you earnestly wish to begin the process of resolving your problem, then stop fearing it! The best chance you will ever have of finding a solution to your problem is to first eliminate the fuel that is keeping it alive. That fuel is none other than your own personal fear.

Although, Fear may not be the problem—it's definitely not the solution. The closest you can get to a solution will come from not fearing the problem.

Fear doesn't eliminate the problem—it only fuels it more! Inviting fear to console you in the midst of a problem is like asking gasoline to come help you put out a fire! Fear is not in the problem-solving business—it never has been and it never will be. However, when people have a problem, they never fail to invite Fear who is the chief anti-solving agent.

When Fear is present, it slams the door in the face of the Holy Spirit! The Holy Spirit and Fear cannot co-exist. The Holy Spirit is God and God doesn't have any alliance with the enemy we call Fear.

Remember, Fear is the devil! When God is **selected**—the devil is **rejected**. But when the devil is selected—God is rejected. Truly, you cannot serve two masters! Thus, when Fear is invited through the front door then the Holy Spirit must leave out the back door. Yet when the Holy Spirit has been invited through the front door then Fear is forced out the back door. It's a revolving door, but the choices are all yours to make!

A New Fear

When you have a new Fear—you have a *new problem* and it will compound with your *old problem*. Now, you have two problems where originally you had just one! Today, you must eliminate both these problems immediately.

If you can get rid of the problem then automatically Fear will be thrown out as well. However, if the problem is going to take time to resolve then Fear must be the *first* to go. **Clearly, you cannot afford to have two enemies, both attacking you at the same time!**

If you have a problem that must be dealt with—you must do all you can to resolve it! However, do not create another adversary. By allowing Fear into your life, you create another adversary! The problem is already bad all by itself—it doesn't need Fear as a personal consultant. Inviting Fear to participate in the finding a solution is like asking the devil to come up with some angelic ideas for the church! It will never happen.

Jesus said: *"How can Satan cast out Satan? (Mark 3:23)."* This simply means: Fear is not an answer for Fear. So please don't compound the problem.

Lesson Ten

Phobia Of Strange Noises, etc.,

Question #2: *When I'm home alone, I periodically hear strange noises and have had lights occasionally and unexplainably go off. Can you explain these strange phenomenons?*

Answer: The first thing you need to understand is that everything has an explanation! You may not be able to explain it, but there is a cause and effect. The other principle of vital importance is: **There Is No Such Thing As A Third World!**

Simply meaning, if you are hearing strange noises or if lights are going on and off—then there is only one of two things, which can explain them. Either it is based solely in the realm of the outer world (man's world) or it is based solely in the the inner world (your imaginary world). Your answer to this problem is within one of these two worlds— guaranteed!

Therefore, if you hear strange noises or see lights strangely going on and off—the very first world you must investigate is the obvious outer world.

As I was writing this book, I experienced a situation just outside my kitchen, where my lights had shut off for a few seconds and then they strangely came back on. The timing of this was ironic as it was the subject matter of this chapter. I could not explain why this was happening and it happened twice! However, I did notice that it only happened when I would plug in my high-powered (3 hp) blender.

Every time I use this machine, it will take some of the electrical power already in use— thereby, causing a reduction of electricity for the lights. **So, that was my answer!** Yet when it happened the first time—it almost threw me back to my ghostly days as a teenager. But thanks to my lessons on Fear—I immediately put out those phobic flames by applying what is called . . .

The Dual World Principle

The dual world principle simply says that all problems are either existing in the outer world or existing within the inner (imaginary) world and there is no other!

The dual world principle emphatically asserts that there are only two worlds, i.e., God's world vs.

devil's world, positive vs. negative, good vs. bad, etc.

Back To The Lights

When we experience on-and-off light occurrences that we cannot explain, it is important not to jump to hasty and bizarre conclusions! Meaning, don't be too quick to blame it on the *spooky world* or some other spooky dynamic. But instead try to figure out the outer world or external reason why those lights are going on and off.

We too often go into a spooky-mode frenzy any time we cannot explain something that appears bizarre, eerie, or strange. We have to really stop this very bad mental behavior.

The mind is a brilliant yet strange and complex creation. The greatest annoyance for the human mind is **"the state of not knowing!"** The mind hates not knowing a thing with a passion!

If the mind cannot explain something—it literally goes into a state of depression. This depression is sometimes so mild in nature that it can easily go undetected, yet in other cases, it can be very obvious.

Since the mind hates not knowing a thing, this is essentially the reason why we, as people, are so inherently NOSEY! We just want to know, have to know and can't breathe properly unless we know something or everything—no matter what it is!

However, something happens when the mind cannot explain an eerie situation. It is already disturbed by the fact that it doesn't have an answer for it. So, when you have a depressed mind hearing unexplained noises—it can really go into a **state of shock** that can clinically be called anxiety or Fear.

How does one eliminate this form of Fear? Essentially, you have to apply *the eagle principle*, which means you have to confront or charge directly into the eye of the storm (fear).

You cannot resolve any problem by avoiding it—as this will only invite the problem more. And so it is the case with this Fear! Meaning, you have to confront it and charge at it with full speed and force until the momentum of this storm (fear) propels you up and above it. The way you must do this is by first preparing your *mind and spirit* before you confront the area or room where the noises appear to be coming from.

Preparing your *mind and spirit* means your spirit must be highly charged and without any fear whatsoever. Fear would simply call your bluff, if you come at him with a cowardly spirit! Thus, your spirit must be filled with great energy, full conviction, and absolute faith. The spirit factor is truly the key in killing fear instantly! So, Please Come With A Strong Spirit!

Next, is the mind factor! The mind's duty is to establish and forcefully **vocalize** the specific and powerful words, which are assigned to call fear's bluff. Here, are the ten most powerful phrases which will eliminate fear in the unexplained lights and noise-department and they must come out in exactly this order:

(1) Are you trying to scare me?
(2) The worst thing that can happen to me is death.
(3) Well, I'm not afraid of death!
(4) So, do you have any more plans?
(5) If not, then stop acting like a little coward and let's talk!
(6) I mean, making noises and playing with lights in an effort to get my attention is what kids and cowards do!

(7) Let me help you out a little bit: If you really want my attention—a conversation will do the trick! So, if you don't want to talk then stop wasting my time!

(8) Coward, it is very and I mean very rude to not answer when somebody is asking you a question! So, not only are you a coward but you have NO MANNERS. Did your parents NOT teach you about respect? I'm very disappointed in you, coward. You really surprised me.

(9) And it's very funny, all the while, I used to be afraid of you. But I never knew that you were this big coward! Look at you; you don't even want to talk. THAT'S A SHAME. I've finally given you what you always wanted, which was my attention and you let me down. Wow, I'm shocked! I'm truly, truly shocked! You really have disappointed me!

(10) Well, I've got to go, COWARD, since you don't feel like talking! (Now you can begin making you way out of the room—for, you have been victorious in this department of Fear!)

CONGRATULATIONS! For, this level of Fear is completely out of your life forever! **The**

eagle principle enabled you to combat, defeat, and win against Fear in this department.

Now, I would like you to seal this victory by reading and studying a quick lesson on . . .

Lesson Eleven

Fear and Logic

The first thing you must understand is that Fear lives in logic! Remember, the lesson: **Discernment is the birthplace of Fear**. Therefore, the more logical you are the more fearful you will become! And anytime your logic cannot explain something that is eerie—it won't be long before the evil baby called Fear is born. Fear is born out of discernment. It is human discernment, which makes Fear real and promotes it from a *state of nothingness* to a *state of somethingness*.

Fear is not *real* without you! For instance, if I were to show you a big house—this house is big with or without you. This house didn't need your discernment to justify how big it is. The house is and will remain BIG whether you agree about its size or not.

However, fear needs your discernment to justify its realness because Fear is not real. Fear is **surreal** (imaginary!). At first, Fear is surreal, but the mind gives it an undue, unfair and unjust promotion and for the very first time—fear becomes real.

What is the meaning of real? **Real** means *Really Existing Affirming Life*. So, when you believe that Fear is *really existing affirming life* then you are in big trouble! And this was the reason why those noises and unexplained lights were so intimidating. It was because to you—they had become *real or really existing affirming life*—within your surreal or imaginary life!

Always remember, Fear needs you to justify who he is! Fear needs you to bring and introduce him into life. Fear is like a presidential candidate—he needs YOU in order for it to be PRESIDENT. I earnestly plead that you do not vote for this evil candidate called FEAR. Don't allow him to get into the big house (your mind) because Fear believes in eternal taxes! Fear seeks to physically, mentally and spiritually tax you to death!

Fear is the worst president in the world! So, don't **vote for him,** that way, you won't have to **cope with him!** Remember, cope means compromise. Compromise means to tenderize. Fear Is Personal Homicide Using The Tool Called **SUICIDE!**

Lesson Twelve

The Fear of Death

"And deliver them, who through fear of death were all their lifetime subject to bondage (Hebrews 2:15)."

Many people have spent their entire lives fearing death. This means that many people have spent their entire lifetime living in bondage!

Fear puts you in this bondage and then the fear of death tags you with a number and places you in a cell. Fear is a maximum-security prison system that is hard to escape, break out or cut loose from!

However, the fear of death is the equivalent to being on **death row!** There is no prison system physically, which has any worse prison conditions than the spiritual prison system within. A physical prison is truly luxurious compared to the wretched conditions of the spiritual prison system within.

There are a lot of people who know how to keep themselves out of physical prisons yet these very same people are *repeat offenders* in the spiritual prison systems within. The recidivism rate in one's spiritual prison is incalculable! Although, you may not have a criminal rap sheet in the physical realm yet your **spiritual rap sheet** is long!

Physically, you are considered a law-abiding citizen but spiritually, You Are A Notorious Outlaw! Physically, you may be crime-free, but spiritually, you are a career-criminal! It is your personal fears that make you a criminal; yet when you fear death, this labels the crime.

"And deliver them, who through fear of death were all their lifetime subject to bondage (Hebrews 2:15)."

We have watched hardened criminals be convicted and sentenced to lifetime terms for heinous crimes. Yet, who sends the innocent man or woman to the prison within? And is he or she really innocent? Who is the judge? And what's the prosecutor's name? Well, the judge, prosecutor, and prisoner are all the *same* person!

Those three people in different positions operating in different capacities—are all the same individual: YOU. But, what is the crime?

A crime is an act, which violates a particular law. Thus, the moment you begin fearing—you open up an entirely new spiritual court session. Once you start having fear for something or about something—**Court Is In Session!**

A spiritual court session starts the moment men and women begin to fear. God's Universal Law demands that we: *"Fear Not!"* The Most High God has NOT given us the spirit of fear.

However, if you should violate such divine law and choose to fear anyway, then you are self-convicted and classified as a criminal, according to this law. Being a criminal doesn't necessarily mean that you are a bad person—it just simply means that you have violated a particular law. And in the case of fear, it is a spiritual violation. This makes you a spiritual criminal according to this spiritual law.

Fear is a sin! **I repeat**; Fear Is A Sin! One more time, FEAR IS A SIN! And to fear death makes you a self-afflicted sinner who will cause your own demise. Now let's go deeper into our subject: Fear of Death.

The Meaning of Death

Death has a *before and after* meaning! If you are still fighting the battle against death then *death* means:

Devil's
Evil
Attempt *to*
Throw *ye in*
Hades (Greek word for Hell)

But if you have *lost* this battle, death means:

Devil
Evilly
Accomplished
This
Hades (Hell)

The Bible is correct; death is not this unfortunate occurrence in life, but it is man's last enemy. Death is only an enemy and the very last one! And as the very last enemy, it doesn't necessarily mean that the enemy should win. No, on the contrary, this enemy called death should lose! We as children of God must see to it that death loses.

As a people, we are famous for saying: *"If it's your time to go then it's your time to go."* **And what time is this?** And who sets the time? We are not wind up clocks! We are human beings created in the image and likeness of God—The God Of Eternal Life—The God, who doesn't take lives but rather grants them and grants them abundantly!

No human being on this planet has a specific **TIMER** assigned to them that regulates how long they will live. Who thought of that nonsense? Was it in your daily newspaper, your favorite monthly magazine, or was it just plain, old-fashioned folklore passed down from generation to generation? In any case, it's all absolutely asinine!

You mean to tell me that the little girl that accidentally dies after being hit by a drunk driver, died because it was her time to go? No, it was those fire drinks (devil spirits) in all that alcohol that influenced this man's ability behind the wheel. And what about the child that is born dead from A.I.D.S.? I guess it was her *time* to go too? And what about the millions of Jews, who died at the evil hands of a crazed maniac, named Hitler? I guess it was their *time* to go too? And what about the millions of Africans, who died in the Middle

Passage as they were being shipped to a terrible life of slavery? I guess it was their *time* to clock out too?

It's very strange how all of these people didn't have the same time *clocking in* (coming in), yet somehow (according to your faulty thinking!) they all had the same time clocking out. That's very strange and to maximize the point even more—that's very stupid!

"My people are destroyed for lack of Knowledge (Hosea 4:6)."

In the case of the little girl who died because of the motorist—the devil made that call. In the case of the small child who was born dead with A.I.D.S.—the devil made that call. For the millions of Jews and Africans who were viciously killed—the devil and his demonic angels made all those calls for causalities too. How dare you say God called all these people to heaven—YOU AND YOUR STUPID RELIGIONS.

If it's your time to go—then it's your time to go!

Again, this is absolute nonsense. Your *time* to go is a devil decision and the role you play is whether you choose to stop him! If the devil wins

THEN YOU DIE! But if you win then **you will live.** Now in spite of all this, God is in the background but he cannot get involved. You may say, why not? It is because God vowed not to impose His Will on man's will.

When man decides to use his will, according to the Will of God, then God can get involved! But until that happens, God has to sit back and watch this battle as it goes down. Your *time* to go is a devil decision and the role you play is whether you choose to stop him!

For centuries and even to this very day, you have people who really believe that God wakes up in the morning with a seriously bad attitude and a death list in his left hand and **zaps you dead** with his right! This is foolishness of the highest level! There is no greater foolishness than this.

Death's New Ruler!

"That through death he might destroy him that had the power of death, that is, the devil (Hebrews 2:14)."

The very powerful key word in this scripture is "**HAD.**" At one time, the devil exclusively governed the entire death department. But we are in the new millennium—the second coming of Christ. Now we have some say, or better yet A LOT OF SAY, in the death department.

The devil doesn't like this power being given to newcomers. He really doesn't! It's like an old politician not willing to give up his seat! But the devil has to go and he (the devil) can take death with him, or we will do it on his behalf.

You may say: *What is God's role in all of this?* God oversees both life and death, but he spiritually supervises just one: LIFE! Thus, everyday of your life you must constantly battle to physically, mentally and spiritually LIVE! And *Fear Not* death because it has NO power over you!

The Story About The Man Who Feared Death

There was once this man who was anxiously ducking death. So, *death* decided to arrive early. Somehow, the apprehensive man got a hunch that *death* would be lurking in his neighborhood in an attempt to have a very important meeting with him. So, the man decided to leave town immediately!

Death finally arrived in town, as scheduled, yet he noticed no one was home. Thus, to kill some time (literally speaking!)—*death* began making its rounds around the town where this man lived and did so at an alarming rate. *Death* even made some unexpected visits to this man's old friends, schoolmates and many other people that he knew and grew up with.

At last, *death* was finally finished with its work in this township (with the exception of the death-ducking man!). Yet before *death* left, he asked the man's neighbor whether she had seen him. The next-door neighbor said: *Yes, she had!* And then, she began telling Death where the man was heading. Death replied: *"That's great because at four o'clock today that is the exact location where I have planned for him to DIE!"*

Then death walked away and with a mischievous smile on his face—he said to himself: *"These type of people truly make my job easy! First, they are already at my office (the place where they shall die). Second, they arrive early (So my coffin for them is already set). Third, I do not have to search for them (because of their fears, they come running to me!). Truly, I love these type of people. Too bad, God doesn't make a lot more of them."*

The moral of the story is: **Just When You Think You Are Running From Death—You're Only Running Smack Into It!**

When you're **not** running from death—it will not even bother to come after YOU! Running from death will only hasten your death. So, don't run from death but instead let death run from the gun called your tongue. The Bible says: *"Death and life is in the power of the tongue (Proverbs 18:21)."* So, if you SAY and BELIEVE that you're not going to die (regardless of what the doctors say) then according to principles of God, YOU WON'T!

The tongue is a highly skillful, spiritual physician and it has kept a lot of sick, sickle cell anemic, cancerous and high blood-pressured people who were scheduled to die from dying.

So, Use Your Tongue! It's a very skillful DOCTOR strapped with a righteous GUN! "For the law of the Spirit of life in Christ Jesus hath made me free from the law of sin and DEATH (Romans 8:2)." Recite this scripture when you are on your deathbed and make that BED come ALIVE!

Death: You Are My Last Enemy.
(And guess what? I'm not afraid of you!)

"The last enemy that shall be destroyed is death."–1 Corinthians 15:26.

Death, you are my last enemy. And guess what? I'm not afraid of you!

Death, you're not *the man* with the gun.
Death, you're *the spirit-man* behind it!

Death, you're not the man who *shoots up the place,*
Death, you're the spirit-man which *started it in the first place.*

Death, I never knew you had a face.
Death, I never knew you had *teeth.*

Death, I never knew you had legs.
Death, I never knew you had *feet.*

Yes, it's all making sense that,
You will need your feet to *flee.*

Death, you are my last enemy. And guess what? I'm not afraid of you!

Death, I thought you came as a *happenstance.*
But death, you *stand* for everything that *happens.*

Death, I always thought you came as an accident!
But death, you're not *an accident;* you're *an incident!*

Death, I never knew you had a face.
Death, I never knew you had *teeth.*

Death, I never knew you had legs.
Death, I never knew you had *feet.*

But, yes, it's all making sense that,
You will need your feet to *flee.*

Death, you are my last enemy. And guess what? I'm not afraid of you!

Death, you're not the *man* behind the mask, who robs.
Death, you're the *camouflage-man* that does this job.

Death, you're not *the man* that rapes her.
Death, you're *the spirit-man* which awaits her.

Death, I never knew you had a face.
Death, I never knew you had *teeth.*

Death, I never knew you had legs.
Death, I never knew you had *feet.*

But, yes, it's all making sense that,
You will need your feet to *flee.*

Death, you are my last enemy. And guess what? I'm not afraid of you!

Death,
It's funny.
I always thought that you were this strange phenomenon, which came upon people unfortunately.

And death,
I always thought that you were just this woeful or fateful occurrence, which strangely happens in a person's life!

But death, I discovered,
you're not just this *strange phenomenon,*
which comes upon people unfortunately.

And death.
you're not just this *woeful or fateful occurrence,*
which strangely happens in a person's life.

But death, you are just an invisible man,
an extremely egregious **EVIL-MAN,**
which is the spirit-man,
secretly tucked underneath
the skin of the physical man. So...

Death,
bring your fight.

Death,
with all your might.

Death,
I'm ready for war.

Death,
rich, middle or poor.

Death,
I'm ready to fight you,

And yes,
even if I have to BITE YOU!

Death,
I HATE YOU to death! And guess what?

I'm Not Afraid of You!

Lesson Thirteen

Fear Is The Greatest Sin!

Fear is man and woman's greatest sin because it absolutely violates God's first commandment! In the book of Exodus, it reads: *"Thou shalt have NO other gods before me (Exodus 20:3)."*

Fear is the devil and the devil is a god, but a terribly evil one. Every time you fear, you are worshipping and paying homage to another god. This is abominable and blasphemous in the eyes of God. The very act of fear infuriates God to such a degree that God places this evil act as rule **number one** in the Ten Commandments!

The Ten Commandments are a prioritized rules and guidelines for all human souls to adhere to. Therefore, to fear would be worse than *murder* because Fear is the worst kind of murder: **Self-murder.** You tell me which is worst: is it the *unrighteous man* that kills because he is EVIL or is it the *righteous man* that kills due to UPHEAVALS (trials of life)?

To murder another is *very, very* bad; yet to murder self is *terribly, terribly* worse!

Lesson Fourteen

Prayer vs. Fear

In prayer, once you ask God for something it is granted! You don't have to hear a voice from God, as God sees and hears all things. Your prayer has given you authority that your request has already been granted.

However, fear comes in to try to make a statement against this authority! Fear says, "*I could care less about that prayer you've just made because you will lose. The worst-case scenario will still occur and there is nothing you can or will be able to do about it!*" This is simply the nature of fear. Fear comes to make a statement against the authority of God, which was granted to you through your prayers. Yet, if fear succeeds in influencing you to doubt the Authority of God then you deserve to be trembling in fear. The most dangerous thing in the world is to put faith in fear! That's dangerous.

What is fear?

Fear is a form of prayer, which goes out to no one but the devil! Can you imagine making a prayer to the devil? However, this is what spiritually happens each and every time you fear. Fear is worshipping this demonic force called Satan. And Satan is nobody except the devil.

Faith vs. Fear

Faith is the spiritual product granted to you through your prayers from God. **Fear** is the spiritual product granted to you through your meditative prayers from the devil. All faiths are signed by the signature of God. Yet all your fears are signed by you and the devil. You are a co-signer with the devil because you contribute to his lie called FEAR.

Therefore, every time you fear—it is a prayer for the devil! And it's a shame when the devil can get more prayers a day than the prayers that go out to God. That's A Shame!

Intense Fear

What is intense fear? Intense fear is nothing more than **an intense prayer** made to the devil. It not only has your name signed to it but also has a spiritual photo of you in color!

Lesson Fifteen

Fear Has Returned!

Be Not Discouraged! Every *Fear Not* student will have moments when fear will raise its ugly head . . . AGAIN! Therefore, I have dedicated this chapter of the book to address the "**ism**" of fear's recidivism, i.c., the backsliders, the repeat-offenders and/or those who have fallen short in the fear preventive department.

Although, one may be educated in the principles of fear, these fear-preventive principles are not yet deeply embedded in one's spirit! Therefore, when you have fallen short in these areas of fear—please refer to this chapter. It is here where I will make an arduous attempt to help you absorb these **fear-preventive principles** firmly into your spirit.

Below are my personal notes, mental tactics and interview excerpts which should be very useful in properly aligning your spirit to destroy the resurgence of fear. You will only need to choose **one** of these aphorisms (sayings), which best empowers your present situation. Next, commit it to memory then close the book!

So, whenever Fear arises, please recite to yourself one of these aphorisms below. And if the aphorism chosen fades or **loses its effectiveness** then return to this chapter and select another one! These sayings are as follow:

- The devil sees your mind as HSN (not the Home Shopping Network), but rather the **House** where **Satan Networks!**

- Doubt, worry, and nervousness are just commercials. But Fear is an infomercial!

- The advertisement of the adversary (the devil) works like this:
  - First, the devil must set his marketing target: **You're The Target!**
  - Second, the devil must create his marketing product: **The Lie Is The Product.**
  - Third, the devil must find a place to advertise: **Your Mind Is The Place.**

Now that the devil has his marketing product and target in place, here's the plan: Advertise, Advertise, Advertise! The devil is only an executive producer of commercials, properly known as evil or fearful thoughts! The devil already knows he cannot make you do anything without your permission. So, the devil spends all of his time advertising these commercials (evil thoughts) until he can persuade you to buy into his lie. If you do not buy into this lie—then it's just pure advertisement: It's Just A Commercial! But if you are **slightly** nervous about the suggestions of the commercial—then this is like pulling out your money, in an *attempt to make* a purchase. However, if you are **extremely** nervous about this commercial—then you have already *purchased* this lie and your receipt, unfortunately, is in the bag (deep in your heart!).

- In the Book of Psalms 52:6 it reads: "*The righteous also shall see, and FEAR, and shall laugh at him.*" Notice the Bible didn't say, "...laugh at it"—the Bible clearly stated, "...laugh at him". Fear is not an "it"—Fear is a "him" (an evil person). The Bible recognizes Fear as a person and so should YOU.

- The people who have Ph.D.'s recognize Fear as an "it". But those blessed with a **Fear Not** Degree recognize Fear as a "him" or as an evil person!

- Those who see Fear as an "it"—are going to *get it!* They will be destroyed!

- Those who see Fear as a "him"—will eventually win. They will become the victor.

- The most dangerous decision to make in the world—is a fearful one!

- The formation of fear is always based on *supposed thinking* or what you have convinced yourself to believe is true. Yet *reality* doesn't have a clue regarding such belief! However, *reality* will welcome this supposed belief and prepare a way to usher it into existence because *reality* has always been a great respecter of deep, concentrated and meditative thought whether positive or negative.

- Fear is formed by taking a mixture of doubts and making false realities out of them.

- Fear is *an information-bound ideology*, which converts into an emotion! So, the minute your information changes so do your emotions. For instance, if I were to insult you with some offensive information (or words)—I could upset your entire emotional state. On the other hand, I could say some very sweet words to you and make you feel very soothed. **It's all in the information!** And we've been given misinformation and disinformation. And disinformation causes the formation of intimidation (or fear).

- Once you clearly understand that fear is *an information-bound ideology* then this is a hundred percent of what the fear-factor consists of but only fifty percent of the problem resolved. The other half is the practical side of identifying and crucifying all the other areas of fear in normal day life.

- *What to do when fear re-appears?*
  Answer: The first thing you must know is that a **fear-problem** is nothing but an **information-problem**. Fear is information GONE BAD! Therefore, if you fix the information—you will also fix the problem: Your Fear Problem.

- **Anytime you go back to fearing—it's because you have misplaced the thoughts that you once used to subdue it!** So, you must recapture those troops (thoughts) so that they can stand as your fortress against the resurgent attack from the forces of fear.

- I think the gravest mistake that educators are making is *advocating copism.* Copism keeps you from seeing fear as an enemy. Once fear has been diagnosed as one's enemy then who advocates coping with an enemy? Your enemy's primary objective is to destroy you! So, identifying fear as the enemy is vitally important and once you've acknowledged him as such then the next step is to destroy him. You must apply the devil's tactics (the enemy's tactics) in reverse. **You Can't Sip Tea With The Enemy!**

- The ultimate goal is to eliminate fear completely. So, I fail to understand copism. Cope means to compromise—compromise means to tenderize. Tenderizing softens the effects of fear. I'm not trying to soften the effects of fear; I'm trying to eliminate them!

- (Interview excerpt) *"What was your overall objective for writing this book?*
Answer: Freedom! This book is the by-product of physical, mental and spiritual freedom. For, there is no greater freedom

than *internal freedom.* Once you've become free from a life of fear—you are unstoppable! Opportunities for success will not just *come* to you—they will *run* to you. Once you've overcome fear, the sky will not look the same; your marriage will not look the same; and as you look around—the world will not look the same. Finally, you are mentally and spiritually free and your physical freedom is only the by-product."

- (Interview excerpt) "There are only a few books which are vitally instructive. This book is one of these, in that it is filled with critical information. But the most important point of this book is not that you will walk away with all the information about fear but it's the feeling you will get after you read this book. You're going to look at life and say, *'What? You mean to tell me that all of this fear stuff was merely a JOKE?'* The feeling of freedom is going to be the most supreme ecstasy you ever had in your life. Money Back Guaranteed! You're going to see fear as fake, phony, false and as silly as the musical group Milli Vanilli. You may even get to the point of being upset for failing to have seen this a long time ago. But the feeling of finally being liberated will immediately overshadow those thoughts."

- (Interview Excerpt) "There's a lot of talk about how we are losing the battle with drugs and how we are losing the battle with A.I.D.S., but we have already lost the battle with FEAR. So, the purpose of this book is to get us back into the "winning column", and after reading this book—you will be an incredible winner!"

- The Bible says, *"And be not conformed to this world: but be ye transformed by the renewing of your mind (Romans 12:2)."* We have to renew our minds and in that process, we have to check for viruses. Viruses or neurological disorders will be present in this process of renewing our minds. Therefore, we have to watch out for them because they make up the foundation of one's fears.

- Overcoming fear is the single greatest human-achievement in the universe. And contrary to popular belief, this is your ONLY objective and greatest achievement! Because once you've defeated this enemy called fear, all of your other objectives will be clearly revealed and very easy to obtain. Unbeknownst to man, we come out of our mothers' wombs predestined to do battle or fight and defeat our greatest enemy. This enemy's name is Fear. Religious people call him the devil but trust me—he's the same spiritual person!

• Once you have won your battle with fear, guess what? Yes, you've just entered into this place called HEAVEN.

• I'm no different from you; I'm a human just like you. But, I have won my battle with my *fear assignment* and it is everyone's duty to win their battle with fear—all their fears. Our education system has never taught that fear was this inborn battle that every man and woman must ultimately face and erase. No, we are taught to keep fear around like comfortable furniture. We are taught to cope with our fears. No, fear has to go! It has to be totally, absolutely and completely eliminated. By far, the worst thing that can ever be taught is to *cope with death*. **Fear is active death using human animations!** So, you can't cope with fear (or ACTIVE DEATH!)—you must eliminate it. The *Fear Not* sciences and teachings point to where fear must go. But traditional teachings on this subject say: *"Make room for fear, just allow it to stay around and everything should be all right."* But everything is not going to be all right— everything is going to be all wrong! And fear will see to it that it is all wrong. If we don't know where to send fear, then that explains why we're so screwed up and why we are losing our battle with fear. Therefore, traditional teaching regarding copism is by far the single most dangerous and damaging doctrine on the planet! And the people teaching it are part of a pool of Ph.D.'s and that is what caused the urgency of this book, *"A Fear Not Degree Is Better Than A Ph.D."*

- So, to hell with trying to win against the Yankees or Los Angeles Lakers, try winning against the lake of fire called fear. That's your biggest and greatest battle. And it's your goal to get yourself in a playoff position against fear and finally take the overall championship. This is the ultimate game of life, which is really not a game because fear *will kill you* (or at least try to!).

- Once you defeat your natural assignment with fear, a coronation of character takes place where a universal unveiling of God's true gifts will be bestowed upon you very abundantly.

- The goal is NOT to master fear—the goal is to master how to fear not!

- This book teaches that fear is not forever, but is temporary! Traditional teaching says, "*Fear is forever*" but this book teaches the exact opposite.

- You are a very special group of people. Everyone is not going to defeat fear but you have to see to it that YOU WILL. The *Feat Not* community is a very small one but it's not discriminatory. You CAN invite yourself and WILL invite yourself once you win against fear.

- With all our intelligence, we still don't know *the purpose of human life*. We still don't know how man should start life, but we all agree on how he should end it—meaning death. We have degrees in the death-department but we're still in nursery school when it comes down to living the abundant life. I just believe that the purpose of life will become crystal clear when one finally defeats the greatest stumbling block that obstructs it—THIS IS FEAR. How can I ever know what's on the other side until I finally remove the thing that blocks its view? You will never see the full view of life when fear has put world-blinders on you.

- The ironic thing is that, we have doctors and clinical therapists who treat symptoms of fear when they should be clients themselves: *I'm like hey, I'm not really following this type of reasoning! I mean it's like, you're trying to explain to me the virtues of not smoking when you smoke three packs a day!*

- I'm a self-experienced expert! And I'm willing to dispute and debate with any so-called expert on this topic. If they're espousing *copism*—I'm *revokism.*

- You can never win the battle against fear while still misdiagnosing it!

- A newborn child has no fear of flying because it can't discern it. However, ten years later, this same child can be very fearful of flying because now it can rationally discern it! Fear is purely informational! If you change the information—you'll change the formation.

- You can determine how close the experts are to devising a resolution for fear by listening to the way in which they still identify it.

- Question: *"Sir, I was sexually assaulted and since then I've been extremely terrified of this happening to me again. Can you tell me how I can overcome such fear?"*
  Answer: As physically, mentally and emotionally traumatizing as it was, do not believe that you will, again, encounter such an unlucky role of the dice! I mean, you just cannot think that badly of yourself. But here's your problem: it is the problem of prevention. Your *natural survival instinct and defensive intuition* are not convinced that you have a safe, secure or attack-proof mechanism in place. And until your natural survival instincts have determined that there exists a satisfactory defense then you will remain arrested by this form of fear. This is the proper diagnosis! This is what people in fear need and that is proper diagnosis. However, you will never be able to get a response like this—or even close to this—if fear is being

misdiagnosed. So, the answer to your question is simple but the process is not.

- There were certain things we've learned in school that many of us will never use in our lifetime like *trigonometry*–however, FEAR was never taught! The most we have learned about FEAR is that it's a four-lettered word and we learned how to spell it. Basically, this is all we've been taught regarding the subject of FEAR.

- Many people create situations to be fearful about! For example, you could be preparing to go to bed. As you lay down and close your eyes, out of nowhere comes a crazy thought like, *"What if someone were to come in and stab me in the back?"* Here, fear wasn't even thinking about you, yet you created a way to find something to fear.

- "People think of ways to invite fear into their lives."

- Fear doesn't really know you by name, but it does have a natural obligation to be your personal adversary. Fear is your spiritual sparring partner preparing you to be the world champion—**Your World Champion Within!**

- Fear is like your universal umbilical cord, in that, once you are saved or born to the principles of righteousness and independent of fear's usage—then it must be DETACHED! And now you are ready to enjoy the fullness of life as God intended.

- Unlike most sparring partners, fear is instructed to kill you—literally! But it is such a tough sparring-session because it is important for you to take him (as well as God's overall purpose for him) seriously! However, God will not permit Satan (fear) to harm you to the extent of death.

- Fear is *False Evidence About Reality—Falsely Envisioning Agonizing Results.* Fear cannot kill YOU. Fear succeeds in killing people only by his deceitful but brilliant illusions. Fear suggests man to walk across the royal, red carpet of life yet the devil fatally rigs this carpet with so many deadly ditches. Thus, man travels such a way and dies!

- Fear cannot kill YOU but he can trick you into killing YOURSELF. However, fear will get the credit as if he did it himself! And you're won't even be alive to set the record straight!

- Fear is a MASTER illusionist! He will illusively lure you to death. Then he will giggle his heart out especially if he's done this to a person who was supposed to be *smart*; or one who has *read* a whole lot of books; or one who has *college degrees* maybe two and especially those with three!

- Fear would have you seeing things that nobody else can see but YOU! Fear is a mirage and an illusion. Fear cannot predict the true aspects of human outcomes. Fear is like a weatherman GONE WRONG! It can't predict the future. So, when a person uses the images that fear projects as reality—this is the gravest mistake one can ever make!

- Fear is a counterfeit receipt to one's belief!

Fear comes out of the world of uncertainty! Whatever you are uncertain about—this is the perfect foundation for fear.

- Uncertainty is the perfect real estate for FEAR to build his house—a haunted house of horror, which certainly will exist within!

- *Uncertainty* is the devil's Garden of Eden! Fear is the evil tree that produces wicked fruit. The wicked fruits of this evil tree are doubt, anxiety, nervousness, worry, scariness, trepidation, intimidation, apprehension, panic-attack, emotional stress, agoraphobia, social phobia, OCD, etc.

- The number one *thought* to help you to regain control of your fears is the thought of abandoning discernment. Remember the lesson, "*Once you start to discern—fear becomes a concern.*"

- I dare you to just abide by these principles without discerning the suggestions of FEAR (the enemy) but trust only in the deliverance of faith. I dare you to be this courageous regarding God's principles.

- Fear is within you and is the devil's way of *spying* on the kingdom of God!

- Last year, the American Institute Of Stress reported that Americans spent over 11.3 billion dollars in therapy—just coping with Fear. When I first learned this news I said to myself, *"Are you serious?* For 11.3 billion dollars you had better do more than just give me a coping solution. For 11.3 billion dollars, you had better have a CURE!

- Therapy should have provided more than just a coping solution for 11.3 billion dollars. However, if all this money didn't go towards a cure then **what was it used for?** Clinically, this has to be one of the worst gross mismanagements of American funds! Who would have ever thought that you (therapists) would be providing yet another aspirin (a temporary relief)? I NEVER HEARD OF AN ASPIRIN, WHICH COST 11.3 BILLION DOLLARS. **This is unfair to the American public!**

- Medication is nothing but an aspirin—it's a temporary relief. So, once your medication wears off, your problem is still the same. A panic-attack victim needs a resolution—not a temporary solution. **Medication only treats symptoms.** Agoraphobia is a symptom;

hypochondria is a symptom; paranoid schizophrenia is a symptom; a panic attack is a symptom but what's the problem? What is the root of the problem? After all this medication and after all this treatment—the ultimate factor remains—you are still paralyzed by your own personal fears. Therefore, you have to go back to the source in order to get answers. Don't go to the symptoms, but go to the source, which is the MIND.

- Once you break the bondage of Fear—you open up a brand **New World!**

- In order to rid our *societies of anxieties*, we have to go to the source.

- Fear is a psychopathological disorder where one concedes that a situation can cause him or her harm and that there is no way to prevent it. You only fear what you cannot prevent. If something is threatening you and if you cannot prevent it—you will develop a fear of it. It is impossible to fear when you're absolutely confident that you can prevent a thing from harming you!

- How can you be an authority on fear when you are just as fearful as the client? It's the same thing that happens in the medical field when doctors are victims of their own diagnoses. **The only true authorities on fear are those who have successfully mastered it!**

- You have to ask yourself, *"Why do these experts, with identical degrees, have vastly different views on the same subject?"*
  Answer: It is because at some point, you have to take that intellectual plunge into the depths of a new doctrine in which your master's or Ph.D. degree **has no authority!** In other words, YOU'RE ON YOUR OWN! And the only things you can rely on NOW are your own raw, natural intuition and intelligence.

- Everyone must win his or her battle with fear. You're not too big for fear. You don't make enough money to the point that you no longer have to concern yourself with fear. Why? It is because FEAR will take all of it, i.e., your house, your car, your boat, your family and will leave you totally bankrupted. Don't play with Fear—Fear will kill you!

- Fear is not going to solve your situation—so why fear it? Faith is the only thing, which can solve your situation—so have faith in it!

- *Do you know what life will be like once you are absolutely, completely and totally fear-free?*
  Answer: Once someone is fear-free, he or she has just attained the highest form of graduation in the human experience. Philosophically, it is referred to as the state of absolute peace. Theologically, it is referred to as the state of heaven. **Fear-free** is heaven and **heaven** is fear-free. This is the ultimate destination of man!

Read The Epilogue and The 15 Lessons Again!

Conclusion:
The Fighter and His Master

The fighter: Master, I won the championship title of the world! My record is now 20-0.

The master: I don't care about what your record is outside of man. What is your record within? You're proud to boast that you are 20-0 but you have 20,000 losses within! In the world, you are regarded as undefeated, but in the spirit world— you are the most defeated. You will greatly impress me when you finally beat your enemy within! When you finally defeat your enemy within, then I will be impressed until then ye shall leave me.

The Fighter Returns 3 ½ Years Later!

The fighter: Master, I have finally defeated and completed all my lessons on human fear!

The master: (as he feverishly kisses him on the forehead says to him) Welcome to heaven on earth! Yes, you good and faithful servant—for, your Lord is truly proud of your entry into His Kingdom.

The End

INDEX

The 12 Laws For The Owner Of This Book

1. Take the wisdom you've learned from this book and share it with others!

2. Take this book with you when you're about to board a plane.

3. Take this book with you if you have to give a speech or a lecture.

4. Take this book with you if you have to act, sing, perform, or entertain.

5. Take this book with you for ALL HOSPITAL VISITS!

6. Read this book whenever you are feeling a surge of anxiety, stress, nervousness, or have butterflies in your stomach.

7. Regard this book as your personal 24-hour Fear Coach!

8. Read this book at least once every month!

9. **LET THIS BOOK BE YOUR NEW BIRTHDAY GIFT TO ALL!** After all, who do

you know that is a master of fear and doesn't need help in the fear, anxiety, and stress-department?

10. WARNING!!! Do not put this book with the rest of your ordinary books. This is not your ordinary book!

11. Read at least one chapter before work or school and one before you go to sleep! This routine will become your daily inner vitamins that will keep you spiritually fit and fearlessly focused.

12. From this day forward regard this not as a book but as your own personal friend! And log on to www.jesussecret.com to meet the rest of your company of friends (books).

Date: TODAY!
To: All Readers.
From: AIM OG.
Re: Feedback!

I'm urging all readers of A *Fear Not Degree Is Better Than A Ph.D.*, to email me with your remarks, comments or compliments, etc., at AIMOG@jesussecret.com. Please state your name, country, state and city along with your comments or compliments and with your consent, I would like to post them on our website! I will await your replies!

Sincerely,

AIM OG

Give The Gift of *A Fear Not Degree Is Better Than A Ph.D.* To Your Friends And Colleagues

Check Your Local Bookstores or Order Your Paperback Copy Here

☐ YES, I want one copy of *A Fear Not Degree Is Better Than A Ph.D.* for $9.95. (N.J. residents add $0.90 tax)

☐ YES, I want two (2) copies of *A Fear Not Degree Is Better Than A Ph.D.* for $17.90. (N.J. residents add $1.44 tax)

☐ YES, I want five (5) copies of *A Fear Not Degree Is Better Than A Ph.D.* for $39.75. (N.J. residents add $3.00 tax)

☐ YES, I want eight (8) copies of *A Fear Not Degree Is Better Than A Ph.D.* for $55.60. (N.J. residents add $3.84 tax)

☐ YES, I want twelve (12) copies of *A Fear Not Degree Is Better Than A Ph.D.* for $71.40. (N.J. residents add $5.40 tax)

☐ YES, I want fifteen (15) copies of *A Fear Not Degree Is Better Than A Ph.D.* for $82.50. (N.J. residents add $6.30 tax)

Include $3.95 shipping and handling for all orders under $50.00. All orders over $50.00 include $6.95 for shipping and handling.

Payment must accompany orders. Allow 5-10 business days for delivery. These books are the **PAPERBACK EDITIONS.**

Make your check or money order payable to:
TruBooks Publishing, LLC
P.O Box 8062
Hillside, New Jersey 07205
www.jesussecret.com

Give The Gift of *A Fear Not Degree Is Better Than A Ph.D.* To Your Friends And Colleagues

Check Your Local Bookstores or Order Your Hardback Copy Here

☐ YES, I want ___ copies of *A Fear Not Degree Is Better Than A Ph.D.* for $18.95 each. (N.J. residents add $1.14 tax)

☐ YES, I want two (2) copies of *A Fear Not Degree Is Better Than A Ph.D.* for $30.00. (N.J. residents add $1.80 tax)

☐ YES, I want five (5) copies of *A Fear Not Degree Is Better Than A Ph.D.* for $75.00. (N.J. residents add $4.50 tax)

☐ YES, I want eight (8) copies of *A Fear Not Degree Is Better Than A Ph.D.* for $100.00. (N.J. residents add $6.00 tax)

☐ YES, I want twelve (12) copies of *A Fear Not Degree Is Better Than A Ph.D.* for $150.00. (N.J. residents add $9.00 tax)

☐ YES, I want fifteen (15) copies of *A Fear Not Degree Is Better Than A Ph.D.* for $175.00. (N.J. residents add $10.50 tax)

Include $3.95 shipping and handling for all orders under $70.00. All orders over $70.00 include $8.95 for shipping and handling.

Payment must accompany orders. Allow 5-10 business days for delivery. These books are the revised **HARDBACK EDITIONS**.

Make your check or money order payable to:
TruBooks Publishing, LLC
P.O Box 8062
Hillside, New Jersey 07205
www.jesussecret.com

Large/Bulk Orders (Paperback)

1) 25 copies of *A Fear Not Degree Is Better Than A Ph.D.*@ $5.25 = $131.25.

2) 50 copies of *A Fear Not Degree Is Better Than A Ph.D.*@ $5.00 = $250.00.

3) 100 copies of *A Fear Not Degree Is Better Than A Ph.D.*@ $4.75 = $475.00.

4) 250 copies of *A Fear Not Degree Is Better Than A Ph.D.*@ $4.50 = $1,125.00

5) 500 copies of *A Fear Not Degree Is Better Than A Ph.D.*@ $4.25 = $2,125.00.

6) 1000 copies of *A Fear Not Degree Is Better Than A Ph.D.*@ $4.00 = $4,000.00.

Please call our 24-hr toll free # 1-800-945-1511 for shipping and handling rates.

The Jesus Secret Series
Presents

Be (lieve) And Behold It Is! by Aim Og $5.95 + S&H $1.95.

Faith: An Unseen Fact. by Aim Og. $5.95 + S&H $1.95.

A Fear Not Degree Is Better Than A Ph.D. by Aim Og $18.95 + S&H $3.95.

*SPECIAL: All Three Books for $19.95 (S & H included!).

We also accept personal checks by phone
Call Toll Free (800) 945-1511
24 hrs, 7 days a week
OR
Make your check or money order payable to:
TruBooks Publishing, LLC
P.O Box 8062
Hillside, New Jersey 07205

www.jesussecret.com

Forth Coming Books:

The Jesus Secret: Part Two! by Aim Og

Thy Father Which Art In Heaven by Aim Og

The Seven Heavens by Aim Og.

Prayer: The Power of the 4, 8, 12's. by Aim Og.

Proverbs of A Man volumes 1 & 2 by Aim Og.

Printed in the United States
69895LV00008B/146